THE TRAGEDY OF
Romeo and Juliet

William Shakespeare

GLOBE BOOK COMPANY

Cover Design: Mike McIver Graphics
Cover Illustration: Richard Martin
Interior Photos: Museum of Modern Art/Film Stills Archive

ISBN: 0-8359-0024-X

Printed in the United States of America.
10   9   8

Globe Fearon Educational Publishers

CONTENTS

ABOUT THE AUTHOR

William Shakespeare was born in Stratford-on-Avon, England, in 1564. It is believed that he attended school there, although there are no records to prove it. Records do show that he married and had children, and that by 1592 he was working as an actor and playwright in London.

During his years in London, Shakespeare belonged to an organization that put on plays. He was one of the company's actors, although apparently not a great star as an actor. Much more important were the plays, 37 in all, that he wrote for the company. In his time, the success of these plays made him a wealthy man.

About 1612, Shakepeare retired from the theater and returned to Stratford. He died there in 1616. After his death, his friends and admirers gathered copies of all his plays and had them published in one volume, the so-called First Folio of 1623. Today these plays stand as the greatest body of writing by one man in the English language, and perhaps in any language.

NOTE ON THE TEXT

In preparing this edition of *The Tragedy of Romeo and Juliet*, we have kept Shakespeare's original language. The following symbol (∗) within the text indicates an abridged passage. All abridged text may be found on pages 24–26 of the Teacher's Manual. We have included extensive footnotes, summaries, and prereading material to make Shakespeare's vocabulary and story accessible to the modern reader.

INTRODUCTION

Perhaps the most famous love story ever written, *Romeo and Juliet* is probably also the most popular romantic tragedy in the English language. It is interesting to know that Shakespeare did not invent the story of Romeo and Juliet. It was already well known and popular when he composed the play sometime around 1594. Shakespeare wrote *Romeo and Juliet* when he was in his late twenties or early thirties, and the picture he painted was a young man's view of young love. In Shakespeare's hands, the story became a beautiful poetic drama, the most lyrical of his tragedies. Even today, his characters Romeo and Juliet represent the perfect example of romantic love to many people.

During the English Renaissance, theater was very popular. The Elizabethan theater itself resembled an open courtyard. The stage was a large platform without a curtain or stage sets. Outdoor scenes or scenes with large numbers of people, such as the brawls and the ball in Romeo and Juliet, occurred in this space. In the center of the stage was a recessed area often set apart by a curtain. This inner stage could serve as an indoor space such as Friar Laurence's cell or the Capulet tomb. Above the stage was a balcony. From here Juliet could speak to Romeo as he waited below in the orchard. Since the stage was without scenery, actors had to depend on words and actions to communicate the setting of a scene. They did have the help of elaborate costumes and props, however. Having no stage sets had one advantage—scene changes could be made very quickly.

During Shakespeare's time, acting companies, called repertory theater companies, staged most of the plays that people saw. An acting company had about fifteen full-time members. Women were not allowed to be on stage. Boys played the women's parts in plays. Playwrights knew the talents of the actors well and often wrote plays created with certain actors in mind. Profits from the performances were distributed among the full members of the company. Shakespeare himself was an actor as well as a playwright and was a part of a successful theater company called The Lord Chamberlain's Men.

The audience came from every level of society. Only wealthier individuals could afford to buy seats. Well-to-do spectators sat in covered galleries around the stage. The rest of the audience stood in the yard around the platform stage. These people were known as groundlings.

As a successful playwright, Shakespeare knew what his audience wanted, and he was an expert in satisfying their needs. The audience demanded action and excitement. They liked their plots bloody and violent. Although the majority of the people could not read, they loved good language. They appreciated the dignity and grandeur of poetry, and they laughed at puns and word games.

What the audience wanted is apparent in the themes of love, death, and disorder present in *Romeo and Juliet*, one of Shakespeare's earliest plays. In this popular tragedy, he included violent action, rowdy humor, and magnificent poetry. At the beginning of the play, Shakespeare told his audience what to expect. The Prologue, which today is usually spoken by a single player, tells of a pair of lovers who die as a result of a feud between their families.

The play is a story of fate and bad luck. The action is swift; the events of the play take place in only five days. Chance brings Romeo to the Capulet feast where he meets Juliet, and they fall in love. Coincidence has Tybalt recognize Romeo and threaten revenge. The Friar sees the lovers' marriage as a lucky turn of events, yet we know it is not. Fate causes Mercutio to take on Tybalt, and fate interferes as Romeo tries to part the combatants. The duel between Tybalt and Romeo becomes inevitable. Even the final tragedy could have been prevented except that fate intervened. Romeo does not receive news of the Friar's plan because of an accident. The Friar reaches the tomb just a moment too late. The play is a series of unlucky events, but Shakespeare has told the story so well that the string of events seems natural.

The characters in *Romeo and Juliet* are entirely true to life. Romeo undergoes several changes as the play progresses. At first, he is a moody youth brooding over an impossible love. After meeting Juliet, he seems to find himself. Throughout the play, Romeo is portrayed as a gentle person, but, when Mercutio is killed, honor forces him to take action. One characteristic of Romeo remains throughout the play: haste and impulsiveness. Like Romeo, Juliet changes through the course of the play. When the play begins, she seems to be a dutiful and obedient daughter. As her love for Romeo grows, she matures into an independent, determined, and courageous adult. The older characters like the Nurse and Old Capulet are not stereotypes but are skillfully created. Each has a distinct personality. The Nurse, one of Shakespeare's most vivid characters, is talkative, earthy, practical, and loving. Old Capulet is quick-tempered, yet strong. Finally, Shakespeare has created an interesting contrast between the five young men in the play: Romeo, Tybalt, Mercutio, Benvolio, and Paris. They are all about the same age and from the same class. By sharply contrasting their personalities, Shakespeare spotlights their individuality.

One of Shakespeare's most popular plays, *Romeo and Juliet* was a success from its first performance. Since then, *Romeo and Juliet* has had a distinguished history of over four hundred years of stage productions. In our own time, it has been presented on film, on television, and, of course, on stage. Shakespeare's "star-crossed lovers" are so unforgettable and vivid that his play has stimulated artists, composers, and choreographers to create works based on the tragedy. It is a play for all people to enjoy.

Dramatis Personae

CHORUS

ESCALUS, *Prince of Verona*
MERCUTIO, *the Prince's kinsman and Romeo's friend*
PARIS, *a young count and kinsman of the Prince*
PAGE *to Count Paris*

MONTAGUE
MONTAGUE'S WIFE
ROMEO, *son of the Montagues*
BENVOLIO, *Montague's nephew and Romeo's friend*
ABRAHAM, *a servant of the Montague household*
BALTHASAR, *a servant of the Montague household attending Romeo*

CAPULET
CAPULET'S WIFE
JULIET, *daughter of the Capulets*
NURSE
TYBALT, *nephew of Capulet's Wife*
PETRUCHIO, *Capulet's kinsman*
SECOND CAPULET, *an old man, Capulet's kinsman*
PETER, *a servant of the Capulet household attending the Nurse*

SAMSON,
GREGORY,
ANTHONY
POTPAN,
CLOWN *or* SERVANT,
Other SERVANTS,
} *servants of the Capulet household*

FRIAR LAURENCE,
FRIAR JOHN,
} *Franciscan friars*

APOTHECARY
Three MUSICIANS *(Simon Catling, Hugh Rebeck, and James Soundpost)*
Three WATCHMEN

Citizens, Maskers, Torchbearers, Guards, Servants, and Attendants

SCENE: *Verona; Mantua*

---◆---

Before You Read The Prologue

The Prologue, which serves as an introduction to the play, previews the action that will take place. This opening speech is really a Shakespearean sonnet with fourteen rhyming lines written in iambic pentameter with a couplet at the end. Shakespeare often used a chorus to sum up or suggest action in his plays.

The Prologue tells the audience that fate is responsible for what happens in this tragedy. Romeo and Juliet are not to blame for their own sad end. They are victims of the quarrel between their families. Their love is "death-mark'd" from the beginning. Why do you think Shakespeare wanted the audience to know about the role fate plays in this play?

---◆---

THE PROLOGUE

[Enter CHORUS]

CHORUS.
>Two households, both alike in dignity, [1]
>>In fair Verona, where we lay our scene,
>
>From ancient grudge break to new mutiny, [2]
>>Where civil blood makes civil hands unclean.[3]
>
>From forth the fatal loins of these two foes
>>A pair of star-crossed lovers take their life; [4]
>
>Whose misadventured piteous overthrows [5]
>>Doth with their death bury their parents' strife.
>
>The fearful passage of their death-marked love, [6]
>
>And the continuance of their parents' rage
>
>Which, but their children's end, naught could remove, [7]
>
>Is now the two hours' traffic of our stage; [8]
>
>The which if you with patient ears attend,
>
>What here shall miss, our toil shall strive to mend. [9]

[Exit]

---

1. **dignity.**   rank, status
2. **mutiny.**   trouble, conflict
3. **Where ... unclean.**   where the blood of some citizens stains the hands of other citizens
4. **star-crossed.**   doomed by bad positions of the stars, fate
5. **misadventured.**   unlucky
6. **passage.**   progress
7. **but.**   except
8. **traffic.**   business
9. **What ... mend.**   If anything is not understandable in this prologue, the actors will try to make it clear in the play.

Before You Read Act I, Scene 1

As the scene opens, a fight breaks out between servants of the Montagues and the Capulets. The violence shows the hostility that exists between the families. This scene also introduces Montague, Capulet, Benvolio, and Tybalt. Notice how much Shakespeare tells you about these characters in only a few lines.

The second part of the scene is about Romeo. After the fight is over, he enters. He is in a gloomy mood over Rosaline, who has rejected him. As you read, decide whether Romeo really loves Rosaline — or just thinks he does. The power of Romeo's love for Juliet is one of the strongest forces in the play. As you read Act I, notice how Shakespeare contrasts the love described in this scene with the love Romeo feels for Juliet. Be aware of how the playwright uses the element of contrast throughout *Romeo and Juliet* to develop and intensify the tragedy.

Shakespeare introduces two other elements in this scene — foreshadowing and an age-youth theme. Notice the Prince's lines that suggest the tragedy to come. The very old feud is between old men, but it will cause the deaths of the youngest members of each family.

ACT I. Scene 1.

Location: Verona. A public place.

[*Enter* SAMSON *and* GREGORY, *with swords and bucklers,* [1] *of the house of* CAPULET]

SAMSON.
Gregory, on my word, we'll not carry coals. [2]

GREGORY.
No, for then we should be colliers. [3]

SAMSON.
I mean, an we be in choler, we'll draw. [4]

GREGORY.
Ay, while you live, draw your neck out of collar. [5]

SAMSON.
I strike quickly, being moved. [6]

GREGORY.
But thou art not quickly moved to strike.

SAMSON.
A dog of the house of Montague moves me.

---

1. **bucklers.**   small shields
2. **carry coals.**   put up with insults
3. **colliers.**   coal sellers
4. **an ... draw.**   If we are angry, we will draw our swords.
5. **collar.**   hangman's noose
6. **moved.**   aroused to anger

GREGORY.

To move is to stir, and to be valiant is to stand. [7]
Therefore, if thou art moved, thou runn'st away.

SAMSON.

A dog of that house shall move me to stand. I will
take the wall of any man or maid of Montague's. [8]
*
GREGORY.

The quarrel is between our masters and us their
men. [9] *Draw thy tool, [10] Here comes of the house
of Montagues.

[*Enter two other servingmen,* ABRAHAM *and
another*]

SAMSON.

My naked weapon is out. Quarrel. I will back thee.

GREGORY.

How, turn they back and run?

SAMSON.

Fear [11] me not.

GREGORY.

No, marry. I fear thee!

---

7. **stand.** stand one's ground
8. **take the wall.** take the cleaner side of the sidewalk
   nearest the wall, thus forcing others out into the gutter
9. **between ... men.** between the males of one
   household and the males of the other household; the
   women would not fight
10. **tool.** weapon
11. **Fear.** mistrust

SAMSON.
Let us take the law of [12] our sides. Let them begin.

GREGORY.
I will frown as I pass by, and let them take it as they list. [13]

SAMSON.
Nay, as they dare. I will bite my thumb [14] at them, which is disgrace to them if they bear it.

[SAMSON *makes taunting gestures*]

ABRAHAM.
Do you bite your thumb at us, sir?

SAMSON.
I do bite my thumb, sir.

ABRAHAM.
Do you bite your thumb at us, sir?

SAMSON.
[*Aside to* GREGORY] Is the law of our side if I say ay?

GREGORY.
[*Aside to* SAMSON] No.

SAMSON.
[*To* ABRAHAM] No, sir, I do not bite my thumb at you, sir, but I bite my thumb, sir.

GREGORY.
Do you quarrel, sir?

---

12. **take the law of.** have the law on
13. **list.** please
14. **bite my thumb.** make an insulting gesture

ABRAHAM.
Quarrel, sir? No, sir.

SAMSON.
But if you do, sir, I am for you. I serve as good a
man as you.

ABRAHAM.
No better.

SAMSON.
Well, sir.

[*Enter* BENVOLIO]

GREGORY.
[*To* SAMSON] Say "better." Here comes one of my
master's kinsmen.

SAMSON.
[*To* ABRAHAM] Yes, better, sir.

ABRAHAM.
You lie.

SAMSON.
Draw, if you be men. Gregory, remember thy washing
blow. 15

[*They fight*]

BENVOLIO.
Part, fools!
Put up your swords. You know not what you do.

---

15. **washing.**   slashing with great force

[*Enter* TYBALT *with sword drawn*]

TYBALT.

What, art thou drawn among these heartless
    hinds? [16]
Turn thee, Benvolio; look upon thy death.

BENVOLIO.

I do but keep the peace. Put up thy sword,
Or manage it to part these men with me. [17]

TYBALT.

What, drawn and talk of peace? I hate the word
As I hate hell, all Montagues, and thee.
Have at thee, coward! [18]

[*They fight*]

[*Enter three or four* CITIZENS *with clubs or
partisans*]

CITIZENS.

Clubs, bills, and partisans! Strike! Beat them
    down! [19]
Down with the Capulets! Down with the
    Montagues!

[*Enter old* CAPULET *in his gown, and his* WIFE] [20]

---

16. **heartless hinds.** cowardly menials
17. **manage.** use
18. **Have at thee.** on guard, here I come
19. **Clubs.** rallying cry, summoning apprentices with their
    clubs. **bills.** long-handled spears with hooked blades.
    partisans. long-handled spears
20. **gown.** nightgown, dressing gown

CAPULET. *old*
   What noise is this? Give me my long sword, ho! 21

CAPULET'S WIFE.
   A crutch, a crutch! Why call you for a sword?

CAPULET.
   My sword, I say! Old Montague is come
   And flourishes his blade in spite of me. 22
   his old, his young

[*Enter old* MONTAGUE *and his* WIFE]

MONTAGUE.
   Thou villain Capulet! — Hold me not; let me go.

MONTAGUE'S WIFE. *wants peace*
   Thou shalt not stir one foot to seek a foe.

[*Enter* PRINCE ESCALUS, *with his train*]

PRINCE.
   Rebellious subjects, enemies to peace,
   Profaners of this neighbor-stainèd steel — 23
   Will they not hear? What, ho! You men, you
      beasts,
   That quench the fire of your pernicious rage
   With purple fountains issuing from your veins, 24
   On pain of torture, from those bloody hands
   Throw your mistempered weapons to the ground 25
   pun not made right
   naughty

---

21. **long sword.** heavy, old-fashioned sword
22. **spite.** defiance, despite
23. **Profaners ... steel.** you who contaminate your
   weapons by staining them with neighbors' blood
24. **purple.** bloody, dark red
25. **mistempered.** having been tempered, or hardened, to a
   wrong use; bad-tempered

And hear the sentence of your movèd prince. [26]
Three civil brawls, bred of an airy word, [27] *no reason*
By thee, old Capulet, and Montague,
Have thrice disturbed the quiet of our streets
And made Verona's ancient citizens
Cast by their grave-beseeming ornaments [28]
To wield old partisans, in hands as old,
Cankered with peace, to part your cankered hate. [29]
If ever you disturb our streets again
Your lives shall pay the forfeit of the peace. [30]
For this time all the rest depart away.
You, Capulet, shall go along with me,
And, Montague, come you this afternoon,
To know our farther pleasure in this case,   *court*
To old Freetown, our common judgment-place. [31]
Once more, on pain of death, all men depart.

[*Exit all but* MONTAGUE, MONTAGUE'S WIFE,
and BENVOLIO]

MONTAGUE.
Who set this ancient quarrel new abroach? [32]
Speak, nephew, were you by when it began? [33]

---

26. **movèd.** angry
27. **airy.** merely a breath, trivial
28. **Cast ... grave-beseeming ornaments.** put aside the
    clothes appropriate to dignified old age
29. **Cankered ... cankered.** corroded . . . malignant
30. **Your ... peace.** death will be the penalty for breaking
    the peace
31. **common.** public
32. **set ... abroach.** reopened this old quarrel
33. **by.** near

BENVOLIO.

Here were the servants of your adversary,
And yours, close fighting ere I did approach.
I drew to part them. In the instant came
The fiery Tybalt with his sword prepared, [34]
Which, as he breathed defiance to my ears,
He swung about his head and cut the winds
Who, nothing hurt withal, hissed him in scorn. [35]
While we were interchanging thrusts and blows,
Came more and more, and fought on part and part [36]
Till the prince came, who parted either part. [37]

MONTAGUE'S WIFE.

O, where is Romeo? Saw you him today? *worried about Romeo*
Right glad I am he was not at this fray.

BENVOLIO.

Madam, an hour before the worshiped sun *before dawn*
Peered forth the golden window of the east, [38]
A troubled mind drave me to walk abroad, [39]
Where, underneath the grove of sycamore
That westward rooteth from this city's side, [40]
So early walking did I see your son.
Towards him I made, but he was ware of me [41]
And stole into the covert of the wood. [42] *hiding from Ben.*

---

34. **prepared.** drawn, ready
35. **Who, nothing.** which not at all. **withal.** therewith.
    hissed. hissed at
36. **on part and part.** on one side and the other
37. **either part.** both parties
38. **forth.** from forth
39. **drave.** drove. **abroad.** outside
40. **that ... side.** that grows on the west side of this city
41. **made.** moved. **ware.** wary, aware
42. **covert.** cover, hiding place

> I, measuring his affections by my own, [43]
> Which then most sought where most might not be
>   found, [44]
> Being one too many by my weary self,
> Pursued my humor, not pursuing his, [45]
> And gladly shunned who gladly fled from me. [46]

MONTAGUE.
> Many a morning hath he there been seen,
> With tears augmenting the fresh morning's dew,
> Adding to clouds more clouds with his deep sighs;
> But all so soon as the all-cheering sun
> Should in the farthest east begin to draw
> The shady curtains from Aurora's bed, [47]
> Away from light steals home my heavy son [48]
> And private in his chamber pens himself,
> Shuts up his windows, locks fair daylight out,
> And makes himself an artificial night.
> Black and portentous must this humor prove
> Unless good counsel may the cause remove.

BENVOLIO.
> My noble uncle, do you know the cause?

MONTAGUE.
> I neither know it nor can learn of him. *He won't tell me*

---

43. **measuring ... affections.** judging his feelings
44. **which ... found.** that wanted a place where I might be alone
45. **humor.** mood, whim
46. **who.** him who
47. **Aurora.** goddess of dawn
48. **heavy.** sad; the opposite of light.

Romeo- always in the dark, depressed

BENVOLIO.
Have you importuned him by any means?

MONTAGUE.
Both by myself and many other friends.
But he, his own affections' counselor,
Is to himself—I will not say how true, [49]
But to himself so secret and so close, [50]
So far from sounding and discovery, [51]
As is the bud bit with an envious worm [52]
Ere he can spread his sweet leaves to the air
Or dedicate his beauty to the sun.
Could we but learn from whence his sorrows grow,
We would as willingly give cure as know.

Hell never find a wife...?

[*Enter* ROMEO]

BENVOLIO.
See where he comes. So please you, step aside. [53]
I'll know his grievance or be much denied.

MONTAGUE.
I would thou wert so happy by thy stay [54]
To hear true shrift. Come, madam, let's away. [55]

[*Exit* MONTAGUE *and his* WIFE]

---

49. **true.** trustworthy
50. **close.** concealed
51. **sounding.** understanding; discovering deep or inner
    secrets
52. **envious.** nasty
53. **So please you.** if you please
54. **happy.** fortunate, successful
55. **shrift.** confession

BENVOLIO.
Good morrow, cousin.[56]

ROMEO.
                    Is the day so young?

BENVOLIO.
But new struck nine.

ROMEO.
                    Ay me! Sad hours seem long.
Was that my father that went hence so fast?

BENVOLIO.   *subtle as a gun*
It was. What sadness lengthens Romeo's hours?

ROMEO.
Not having that which, having, makes them short.

BENVOLIO.
In love?

ROMEO.
Out —

BENVOLIO.
Of love?

ROMEO.   *he loves her she doesn't love him*
Out of her favor where I am in love.

BENVOLIO.
Alas, that Love, so gentle in his view, [57]
Should be so tyrannous and rough in proof! [58]

---

56. cousin. kinsman
57. his view. its appearance
58. in proof. in reality, in experience

ROMEO.

Alas, that Love, whose view is muffled still, [59]
Should without eyes see pathways to his will! [60]
Where shall we dine? —O me! What fray was
    here?   *annoyed with feud*
Yet tell me not, for I have heard it all.
Here's much to do with hate, but more with love. [61]
Why, then, O brawling love, O loving hate, *easy*
O anything of nothing first create,   *hate is hard*
O heavy lightness, serious vanity,   *love is hard*
Misshapen chaos of well-seeming forms,
Feather of lead, bright smoke, cold fire, sick
    health,
Still-waking sleep, that is not what it is! [62]
This love feel I, that feel no love in this.
Dost thou not laugh?

BENVOLIO.

No, coz, I rather weep. [63]

ROMEO.

Good heart, at what?

BENVOLIO.
                          I feel sorry for you
At thy good heart's oppression.

ROMEO.

Why, such is love's transgression.

---

59. **view ... still.** sight is blindfolded always
60. **to his will.** to what he wants
61. **but ... love.** loyalty to family and love of fighting.
    Romeo is talking about the contradictions of love.
62. **Still-waking.** continually awake
63. **coz.** cousin, kinsman

Doesn't
want Ben
to feelbad

Griefs of mine own lie heavy in my breast,
Which thou wilt propagate, to have it pressed
With more of thine. This love that thou hast
    shown [64]
Doth add more grief to too much of mine own.
Love is a smoke made with the fume of sighs;
Being purged, a fire sparkling in lovers' eyes; [65]
Being vexed, a sea nourished with lovers' tears.
What is it else? A madness most discreet, [66]
A choking gall, and a preserving sweet. [67]
Farewell, my coz.

BENVOLIO.
                    Soft! I will go along. [68]
An if you leave me so, you do me wrong. [69]

ROMEO.
    Tut, I have lost myself. I am not here.
    This is not Romeo; he's some other where.

BENVOLIO.
    Tell me in sadness, who is that you love? [70]

ROMEO.
    What, shall I groan and tell thee?

BENVOLIO.
                    Groan? Why, no,

---

64. **propagate ... thine.** increase by having it, my own
    grief, increased by your grief on my account
65. **purged.** cleansed of smoke
66. **discreet.** careful
67. **gall.** bitter liquid
68. **Soft.** wait a moment
69. **An if.** if
70. **sadness.** seriousness. **is that.** is it whom

But sadly tell me who. [71]

ROMEO.
Bid a sick man in sadness make his will —
A word ill urged to one that is so ill! [72]
In sadness, cousin, I do love a woman.

BENVOLIO. *No dub*
I aimed so near when I supposed you loved.

ROMEO.
A right good markman! And she's fair I love. [73]

BENVOLIO.
A right fair mark, fair coz, is soonest hit. [74] *shall be taken soon.*

ROMEO.
Well, in that hit you miss. She'll not be hit
With Cupid's arrow. She hath Dian's wit, [75]
And, in strong proof of chastity well armed, [76]
From love's weak childish bow she lives unharmed.
She will not stay the siege of loving terms, [77] *no love letters*
Nor bide th' encounter of assailing eyes, [78] *no puppy dog eyes*
Nor ope her lap to saint-seducing gold. *no jewelry*
O, she is rich in beauty, only poor
That when she dies, with beauty dies her store. [79] *no children to pass her beauty to*

---

71. **sadly.** seriously
72. **A word.** sadly or in sadness — too sad a word, says
    Romeo, for a melancholy lover
73. **fair.** beautiful
74. **fair mark.** clear, distinct target
75. **Dian.** Diana, huntress and goddess of chastity
76. **proof.** armor
77. **stay.** submit to
78. **bide.** endure, put up with
79. **That ... store.** She will die without children and
    therefore her beauty will die with her.

BENVOLIO.
Then she hath sworn that she will still live chaste? [80]

ROMEO.
She hath, and in that sparing makes huge waste, [81]
For beauty starved with her severity
Cuts beauty off from all posterity. [82]
She is too fair, too wise, wisely too fair,
To merit bliss by making me despair. [83]
She hath forsworn to love, and in that vow [84]
Do I live dead that live to tell it now.

BENVOLIO.
Be ruled by me. Forget to think of her.

ROMEO.
O, teach me how I should forget to think!

BENVOLIO.
By giving liberty unto thine eyes:
Examine other beauties. *Other fish in the sea*

ROMEO.
                    'Tis the way *they'll make her look more beautiful*
To call hers, exquisite, in question more. [85]
These happy masks that kiss fair ladies' brows,

---

80. **still.** always
81. **sparing.** stinginess
82. **For ... posterity.** By refusing love and marriage, she
    wastes her beauty, because it will not be passed on to
    future generations.
83. **To ... despair.** earning her own salvation through
    chaste living while dooming me to live without
    her love
84. **forsworn to.** renounced, rejected
85. **in question more.** even more strongly to mind,
    into consideration

Being black, puts us in mind they hide the fair.
He that is strucken blind cannot forget
The precious treasure of his eyesight lost.
Show me a mistress that is passing fair: [86]
What doth her beauty serve but as a note
Where I may read who passed that passing fair? [87]
Farewell. Thou canst not teach me to forget.

BENVOLIO.
I'll pay that doctrine, or else die in debt. [88]

[Exit]

---

86. passing. surpassingly
87. passed. surpassed
88. pay that doctrine. give that instruction.
   die in debt. feel I've failed as a friend

---◆---

Synopsis of Act I, Scene 1

In the last scene, servants of the Montagues and the Capulets began a fight just as Benvolio and Tybalt entered. Although Benvolio tried to stop the brawl, Tybalt challenged him to fight. When the heads of the Capulet and Montague families came on the scene, they too wanted to fight. However, the Prince of Verona stopped the fighting and declared if the peace was broken again, both men would be executed.

After the others left, Benvolio, Montague, and Lady Montague expressed concern about Romeo's moody behavior. All three were naturally worried about him. Romeo revealed to Benvolio that he was hopelessly in love. Benvolio suggested that he get over Rosaline by comparing her to other girls.

---◆---

Before You Read Act I, Scene 2

Two sets of conversations create contrast in Scene 2. One is between Capulet and Paris; the other is between Romeo and Benvolio. In the first conversation, Capulet tells how precious Juliet is to him. Notice how his dialogue echoes the age-youth theme of Scene 1. Shakespeare also shows us Paris's respectful and proper character, which will contrast with Romeo's recklessness. Soon Romeo will break all the rules to be with Juliet. Finally, notice that fate is creating the opportunity for Romeo to meet Juliet. How do you think they will meet?

ACT I. Scene 2.

Location: Verona. A street.

[*Enter* CAPULET, COUNTY PARIS, *and* THE CLOWN, (A SERVINGMAN)] [1]

CAPULET.
But Montague is bound as well as I, [2]
In penalty alike, and 'tis not hard, I think,
For men so old as we to keep the peace.

PARIS.
Of honorable reckoning are you both, [3]
And pity 'tis you lived at odds so long.
But now, my lord, what say you to my suit?

CAPULET.
But saying o'er what I have said before. [4]
My child is yet a stranger in the world;
She hath not seen the change of fourteen years.
Let two more summers wither in their pride
Ere we may think her ripe to be a bride.

PARIS.
Younger than she are happy mothers made.

CAPULET.
And too soon marred are those so early made.
The earth hath swallowed all my hopes but she; [5]

---

1. **County.** Count
2. **bound.** legally obligated (to keep the peace)
3. **reckoning.** estimation, reputation
4. **o'er.** again
5. **hopes.** children

She's the hopeful lady of my earth. [6]
But woo her, gentle Paris, get her heart; *Make her love you*
My will to her consent is but a part; *choice*
And, she agreed, within her scope of choice [7]
Lies my consent and fair according voice.
This night I hold an old accustomed feast, [8]
Whereto I have invited many a guest
Such as I love; and you among the store, [9]
One more, most welcome, makes my number more.
At my poor house look to behold this night
Earth-treading stars that make dark heaven light. [10]
Such comfort as do lusty young men feel [11] *"Find someone*
When well-appareled April on the heel [12] *else"*
Of limping winter treads, even such delight
Among fresh fennel buds shall you this night [13]
Inherit at my house. Hear all, all see, [14]
And like her most whose merit most shall be;
Which on more view of many, mine, being one, [15]
May stand in number, though in reckoning none.

Doesn't want to lose her

---

6. **the hopeful ... earth.** my heir and hope for posterity.
   (Earth includes property and lands.)
7. **she ... voice.** If she agrees, I will consent to her choice.
8. **old accustomed.** traditional
9. **store.** group
10. **Earth-treading stars.** young women
11. **lusty.** lively
12. **well-appareled.** newly clothed in green
13. **fennel.** flowering herb thought to have the power of
    awakening passion
14. **Inherit.** possess
15. **Which ... none.** When you have looked over all the
    young girls, you might see my daughter as one of the
    many and not as someone special.

Come, go with me. [*To the* SERVINGMAN, *giving
   a paper*]
                    Go, sirrah, trudge about [16]
Through fair Verona; find those persons out
Whose names are written there, and to them say,
My house and welcome on their pleasure stay. [17]

                    [*Exit, with* PARIS]

SERVINGMAN.
Find them out whose names are written here! It is
written that the shoemaker should meddle with his
yard [18] and the tailor with his last, the fisher with his
pencil, and the painter with his nets; but I am sent to
find those persons whose names are here writ, and
can never find [19] what names the writing person hath
here writ. I must to the learned. — In good time! [20]

[*Enter* BENVOLIO *and* ROMEO]

BENVOLIO.
Tut, man, one fire burns out another's burning,

---

16. **sirrah.** (customary form of address to servants)
17. **on ... stay.** wait to serve their pleasure
18. **yard, last, pencil, nets.** The servingman humorously
    assigns these tools of a trade to the wrong person, to
    suggest how useless it is for him, an illiterate servant, to
    be given a written instruction. **yard.** yardstick.
    last. a shoemaker's form. **pencil.** paint brush
19. **find ... find.** locate ... learn
20. **in good time.** here comes help

One pain is lessened by another's anguish; [21]
Turn giddy, and be holp by backward turning; [22]
One desperate grief cures with another's languish. [23]
Take thou some new infection to thy eye,
And the rank poison of the old will die. [24]

ROMEO.
Your plantain leaf is excellent for that. [25]

BENVOLIO.
For what, I pray thee?

ROMEO.
For your broken shin.

BENVOLIO.
Why, Romeo, art thou mad?

ROMEO.
Not mad, but bound more than a madman is; [26]
Shut up in prison, kept without my food,
Whipped and tormented and — Good e'en, good
    fellow. [27]

SERVINGMAN.
God gi' good e'en. I pray, sir, can you read? [28]

---

21. **another's anguish.** the anguish of another pain
22. **holp.** helped. **backward.** reverse
23. **cures ... languish.** is cured by the suffering of a
    second grief or pain
24. **rank.** stinking
25. **plantain leaf.** herb used for cuts and abrasions, such
    as a broken or bleeding shin
26. **bound.** the usual treatment for madness
27. **Good e'en.** good evening
28. **gi'.** give you

ROMEO.

Ay, mine own fortune in my misery.

SERVINGMAN.

Perhaps you have learned it without book. [29]
But, I pray, can you read anything you see?

ROMEO.

Ay, if I know the letters and the language.

SERVINGMAN.

Ye say honestly. Rest you merry! [30]

[*Going*]

ROMEO.

Stay, fellow, I can read.
[*He reads the letter*]
"Signor Martino and his wife and daughters,
County Anselme and his beauteous sisters,
The lady widow of Vitruvio,
Signor Placentio and his lovely nieces,
Mercutio and his brother Valentine,
Mine uncle Capulet, his wife, and daughters,
My fair niece Rosaline, and Livia,
Signor Valentio and his cousin Tybalt,
Lucio and the lively Helena."
A fair assembly. Whither should they come? [31]

---

29. **without book.** By memory; the servingman takes
Romeo's flowery response to his question as though it were
the title of a literary work; his comment also suggests that
people can learn about misery without knowing how to read.
30. **Rest you merry.** farewell
31. **Whither.** where

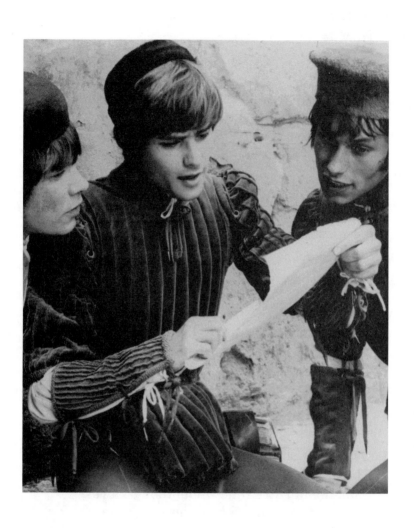

SERVINGMAN.
Up.

ROMEO.
Whither? To supper?

SERVINGMAN.
To our house.

ROMEO.
Whose house?

SERVINGMAN.
My master's.

ROMEO.
Indeed, I should have asked thee that before.

SERVINGMAN.
Now I'll tell you without asking. My master is the
great rich Capulet; and if you be not of the house of
Montagues, I pray, come and crush [32] a cup of wine.
Rest you merry!

[*Exit*]

BENVOLIO.
At this same ancient feast of Capulet's [33]
Sups the fair Rosaline whom thou so loves,
With all the admirèd beauties of Verona.
Go thither, and with unattainted eye [34]
Compare her face with some that I shall show,
And I will make thee think thy swan a crow.

---

32. **crush.** drink
33. **ancient.** customary
34. **unattainted.** unbiased, objective

ROMEO.

When the devout religion of mine eye
Maintains such falsehood, then turn tears to fires; [35]
And these who, often drowned, could never die, [36]
Transparent heretics, be burnt for liars! [37]
One fairer than my love? The all-seeing sun
Ne'er saw her match since first the world begun.

BENVOLIO.

Tut, you saw her fair, none else being by,
Herself poised with herself in either eye; [38]
But in that crystal scales let there be weighted [39]
Your lady's love against some other maid
That I will show you shining at this feast,
And she shall scant show well that now seems best. [40]

ROMEO.

I'll go along, no such sight to be shown,
But to rejoice in splendor of mine own. [41]

[*Exit*]

---

35. **Maintains.** upholds
36. **these.** these my eyes. **drowned.** in tears
37. **Transparent.** self-evident; clear
38. **poised.** balanced
39. **crystal scales.** Romeo's eyes are scales in which the young women are to be balanced and compared.
40. **scant.** scarcely, barely
41. **mine own.** the sight of my own Rosaline

———————◆———————

Synopsis of Act I, Scene 2

In Scene 2, the County Paris asked Capulet for Juliet's hand in marriage. Her father thought she was too young. However, if Juliet agreed, Capulet would give his consent.

Fate entered the picture when the illiterate servant, sent by Capulet to invite people to a feast, asked Romeo to read the guest list. Benvolio and Romeo decided to crash the party. Benvolio hoped to cure Romeo of Rosaline, and Romeo hoped to see his lady love.

———————◆———————

---◆---

Before You Read Act I, Scene 3

As we first meet Juliet, she seems quiet and obedient. However, she, like Romeo, will change. In fact, Shakespeare hints at her later rebelliousness in this scene. Notice Juliet's speech that reveals she will not obey her parents blindly and without question.

In contrast to a formal Lady Capulet, the Nurse is open, frank, and casual, even a little vulgar. Notice that her outspoken comments will run throughout the play to balance and contrast with the growing tragedy. Why do you think Shakespeare created characters like the Nurse?

---◆---

ACT I. Scene 3.

Location: Verona. Capulet's house.

[*Enter* CAPULET'S WIFE *and* NURSE]

WIFE.
Nurse, where's my daughter? Call her forth to me.

NURSE.
  *
I bade her come. What, lamb! What, ladybird! [1]
God forbid. Where's this girl? What, Juliet!

[*Enter* JULIET]

JULIET.
How now? Who calls?

NURSE.
Your mother.

JULIET.
Madam, I am here. What is your will?

WIFE.
This is the matter. — Nurse, give leave awhile, [2]
We must talk in secret. — Nurse, come back again;
I have remembered me, thou's hear our counsel. [3]
Thou knowest my daughter's of a pretty age.

NURSE.
Faith, I can tell her age unto an hour.

---

1. **What.** an expression of impatience. **ladybird.**
    sweetheart
2. **give leave.** leave us
3. **thou's.** thou shalt

WIFE.
> She's not fourteen.

NURSE.
>>   I'll lay fourteen of my teeth —
> And yet, to my teen be it spoken, I have but four — 4
> She's not fourteen. How long is it now
> To Lammastide? 5

WIFE.
>>   A fortnight and odd days.

NURSE.
> Even or odd, of all days in the year,
> Come Lammas Eve at night shall she be fourteen.
> Susan and she — God rest all Christian souls! — 6
> Were of an age. Well, Susan is with God;
> She was too good for me. But, as I said,
> On Lammas Eve at night shall she be fourteen,
> That shall she, marry, I remember it well. 7
> 'Tis since the earthquake now eleven years.
> *
> Thou wast the prettiest babe that e'er I nursed.
> An I might live to see thee married once, 8
> I have my wish.

WIFE.
> Marry, that "marry" is the very theme
> I came to talk of. Tell me, daughter Juliet,
> How stands your disposition to be married? 9

---

4. **teen.** sorrow
5. **Lammastide.** the days near August 1
6. **Susan.** the Nurse's own child who has evidently died
7. **marry.** by the virgin Mary
8. **once.** someday
9. **disposition.** inclination, feelings about being married

JULIET.
It is an honor that I dream not of.

WIFE. *polite*
Well, think of marriage now. Younger than you
Here in Verona, ladies of esteem [10]
Are made already mothers. By my count
I was your mother much upon these years [11]
That you are now a maid. Thus then in brief:
The valiant Paris seeks you for his love.

NURSE.
A man, young lady! Lady, such a man
As all the world — why, he's a man of wax. [12]

WIFE.
Verona's summer hath not such a flower.

NURSE.
Nay, he's a flower, in faith, a very flower. [13]

WIFE.
What say you? Can you love the gentleman?
This night you shall behold him at our feast.
Read o'er the volume of young Paris' face
And find delight writ there with beauty's pen;
Examine every married lineament [14]
And see how one another lends content, [15]
And what obscured in this fair volume lies

---

 9. **disposition.** inclination, feelings about being married
10. **esteem.** high position, nobility
11. **much ... years.** at about the same age
12. **a man of wax.** handsome, a model of wax
13. **Nay.** indeed
14. **married.** harmonized   **lineament.** facial feature

Find written in the margent of his eyes. [16]
This precious book of love, this unbound lover, [17]
To beautify him, only lacks a cover. [18]
The fish lives in the sea, and 'tis much pride [19]
For fair without the fair within to hide.
That book in many's eyes doth share the glory [20]
That in gold clasps locks in the golden story;
So shall you share all that he doth possess,
By having him, making yourself no less.

[handwritten margin note: Love me from fairy tales no experience]

NURSE.
No less? Nay, bigger. Women grow by men.

WIFE.
Speak briefly: can you like of Paris' love? [21]

JULIET.
I'll look to like, if looking liking move, [22]
But no more deep will I endart mine eye [23]
Than your consent gives strength to make it fly.

[handwritten margin notes: Doesn't believe in love at first sight; obedient]

---

15. **content.** satisfaction; substance
16. **margent.** commentary or marginal notes
17. **unbound.** because not bound in marriage (with a double meaning in the continuing metaphor of an unbound book)
18. **a cover.** marriage, a wife
19. **The fish ... hide.** The fish has its proper environment, and simlarly in the environment of marriage Juliet would complement Paris.
20. **That book ... story.** For many people a good story is all the more admirable for being attractively bound. **clasps.** bookfastenings; embraces
21. **like of.** be pleased with
22. **liking move.** may provoke affection
23. **endart mine eye.** let my eyes shoot Love's darts

[*Enter* SERVINGMAN]

SERVINGMAN.
Madam, the guests are come, supper served up, you
called, my young lady asked for, the Nurse cursed [24]
in the pantry, and everything in extremity. I must
hence to wait. I beseech you, follow straight. [25]

WIFE.
We follow thee. [*Exit* SERVINGMAN] Juliet, the
County stays. [26]

NURSE.
Go, girl, seek happy nights to happy days.

[*Exit*]

---

24. cursed. for not helping with the preparations
25. straight. at once
26. County stays. Count Paris waits for you.

———————◆———————

Synopsis of Act I, Scene 3

Juliet listened as Lady Capulet brought up the subject of marriage. Juliet was not excited about the idea for she had never been in love. The Nurse, however, thought Paris was perfect. Juliet showed a hint of independence for she promised only to look and see if she might like the County. Before the conversation could go further, a servant announced the guests had arrived.

———————◆———————

---◆---

Before You Read Act I, Scene 4

Meanwhile, Romeo, Mercutio, Benvolio and other masked companions stroll to the feast. Observe how all the threads of the plot are being woven together. There is the feud between the families. Romeo has a romantic nature. Paris has talked with Capulet about marriage to Juliet. Romeo has the accidental opportunity to attend the Capulet's feast. Juliet is young and innocent. Taken together all these facts suggest that there will be a tragedy. Notice how suspense builds as Romeo and his companions travel to the Capulet palace.

---◆---

ACT I. Scene 4.

Location: Verona. A street in the vicinity of Capulet's house.

[*Enter* ROMEO, MERCUTIO, BENVOLIO, *with five or six other maskers; torchbearers*]

ROMEO.
What, shall this speech be spoke for our excuse? [1]
Or shall we on without apology? [2]

BENVOLIO.
The date is out of such prolixity. [3]
We'll have no Cupid hoodwinked with a scarf, [4]
Bearing a Tartar's painted bow of lath, [5]
Scaring the ladies like a crowkeeper; [6]
Nor no without-book prologue, faintly spoke [7]
After the prompter, for our entrance;
But, let them measure us by what they will,
We'll measure them a measure, and be gone. [8]

Don't tell anyone

---

1. **speech.** Maskers were customarily announced by a messenger with a speech full of compliments.
2. **on.** go on, approach
3. **The date ... prolixity.** Such wordiness is out of fashion.
4. **Cupid.** messenger or "presenter," probably a boy, disguised as Cupid. **hoodwinked.** blindfolded
5. **Tartar's ... bow.** Tartar's bows, shorter and more curved than the English longbow, resembled the old Roman bow which Cupid often carried. **lath.** flimsy wood
6. **crowkeeper.** scarecrow
7. **without-book.** memorized
8. **measure ... measure.** perform a dance for them

ROMEO.

Give me a torch. I am not for this ambling.
Being but heavy, I will bear the light. 9

MERCUTIO.

Nay, gentle Romeo, we must have you dance.

ROMEO.

Not I, believe me. You have dancing shoes
With nimble soles; I have a soul of lead
So stakes me to the ground I cannot move.

MERCUTIO.

You are a lover; borrow Cupid's wings
And soar with them above a common bound. 10

ROMEO.

I am too sore enpiercèd with his shaft 11
To soar with his light feathers, and so bound 12
I cannot bound a pitch above dull woe. 13
Under love's heavy burden do I sink.

MERCUTIO.

And, to sink in it, should you burden love — 14
Too great oppression for a tender thing.

ROMEO.

Is love a tender thing? It is too rough,

---

9. **heavy.** sad; the opposite of light
10. **common.** ordinary. **bound.** leap in the dance; limit
11 . **sore.** sorely
12. **bound.** confined
13. **pitch.** height; a term from falconry for the highest point
of a hawk's flight
14. **to sink ... love.** If you should sink in love, you would
burden it.

Too rude, too boisterous, and it pricks like thorn.

MERCUTIO.
If love be rough with you, be rough with love.
*
Give me a case to put my visage in. [15]

[*He puts on a mask*]

A visor for a visor! What care I [16]
What curious eye doth quote deformities? [17]
Here are the beetle brows shall blush for me.

BENVOLIO.
Come knock and enter, and no sooner in
But every man betake him to his legs. [18]

ROMEO.
A torch for me. Let wantons light of heart
Tickle the senseless rushes with their heels, [19]
For I am proverbed with a grandsire phrase: [20]
I'll be a candle holder and look on. [21]
The game was ne'er so fair, and I am done. [22]

---

15. **case.** mask
16. **A visor ... visor.** a mask for a face with ugly features
17. **quote.** notice
18. **to his legs.** to dancing
19. **Let ... rushes.** let fun-loving people dance on the
    floor covering
20. **proverbed ... phrase.** furnished with an old proverb
21. **candle holder.** onlooker
22. **The game ... done.** No matter how much fun people are
    having, Romeo will have none.

MERCUTIO.
> Tut, dun's the mouse, the constable's own word. [23]
> If thou art dun, we'll draw thee from the mire
> Of — save your reverence — love, wherein thou
>   stickest [24]
> Up to the ears. Come, we burn daylight, ho! [25]

ROMEO.
> Nay, that's not so.

MERCUTIO.
>   I mean, sir, in delay
> We waste our lights in vain, like lamps by day.
> Take our good meaning, for our judgment sits [26]
> Five times in that ere once in our five wits.

ROMEO.
> And we mean well in going to this masque,
> But 'tis no wit to go. [27]

MERCUTIO.
>   Why, may one ask?

---

23. **dun's the mouse.** "keep still." Dun also alludes to
    a Christmas game, "Dun [the gray-brown horse] is in the
    mire," in which a heavy log representing a horse was
    hauled out of an imaginary mire by the players.
    constable's own word. A constable might say "Keep
    still" while waiting to make an arrest.
24. **save your reverence.** An apology for an improper
    expression, which Mercutio supposes "love" to be.
25. **burn daylight.** waste time
26. **Take ... wits.** Try to understand what I mean to say,
    relying on common sense and intelligence rather than on
    your senses.
27. **wit.** wisdom

ROMEO.
I dreamt a dream last night.

MERCUTIO.
And so did I.

ROMEO.
Well, what was yours?

MERCUTIO.
That dreamers often lie.

ROMEO.
In bed asleep, while they do dream things true.

MERCUTIO.
O, then, I see Queen Mab hath been with you. [28]
She is the fairies' midwife, and she comes
In shape no bigger than an agate stone [29]
On the forefinger of an alderman, [30]
Drawn with a team of little atomi [31]
Over men's noses as they lie asleep.
Her chariot is an empty hazelnut,
Made by the joiner squirrel or old grub, [32]
Time out o' mind the fairies' coachmakers.
Her wagon spokes made of long spinners' legs, [33]
The cover of the wings of grasshoppers,

---

28. **Queen Mab.** a name for the Fairy Queen
29. **agate stone.** precious stone often carved with tiny figures and set in a ring
30. **alderman.** member of the municipal council
31. **atomi.** tiny creatures (atoms)
32. **joiner.** furniture maker. **grub.** insect larva which bores holes in nuts
33. **spinners'.** spiders'

Her traces of the smallest spider web,
Her collars of the moonshine's watery beams,
Her whip of cricket's bone, the lash of film, 34
Her wagoner a small gray-coated gnat, 35
Not half so big as a round little worm 36
Pricked from the lazy finger of a maid.
And in this state she gallops night by night 37
Through lovers' brains, and then they dream of
      love;
O'er courtiers' knees, that dream on curtsies
      straight; 38
O'er lawyers' fingers, who straight dream on fees;
O'er ladies' lips, who straight on kisses dream,
Which oft the angry Mab with blisters plagues
Because their breaths with sweetmeats tainted
      are. 39
Sometimes she gallops o'er a courtier's nose,
And then dreams he of smelling out a suit. 40
And sometimes comes she with a tithe-pig's tail 41
Tickling a parson's nose as 'a lies asleep;
Then dreams he of another benefice. 42
Sometimes she driveth o'er a soldier's neck,

---

34. **film.** spider's thread
35. **wagoner.** chariot driver
36. **worm.** refers to an ancient superstition that "worms
      breed in the fingers of the idle"
37. **state.** pomp, dignity
38. **curtsies.** bows. **straight.** immediately
39. **sweetmeats.** candies or candied preserves
40. **smelling ... suit.** finding someone who has a petition for
      the king and who will pay for the courtier's influence
      at court
41. **tithe-pig.** pig given to the parson instead of money
42. **benefice.** a church job that includes an income

And then dreams he of cutting foreign throats,
Of breaches, ambuscadoes, Spanish blades, [43]
Of healths five fathom deep, and then anon [44]
Drums in his ear, at which he starts and wakes,
And being thus frighted swears a prayer or two
And sleeps again. This is that very Mab
That plats the manes of horses in the night, [45]
And bakes the elflocks in foul sluttish hairs, [46]
Which once untangled much misfortune bodes.
This is the hag, when maids lie on their backs,
That presses them and learns them first to bear, [47]
Making them women of good carriage. [48]
This is she —

ROMEO.
            Peace, peace, Mercutio, peace!
Thou talk'st of nothing.

MERCUTIO.
            True, I talk of dreams,
Which are the children of an idle brain,
Begot of nothing but vain fantasy, [49]

---

43. **breaches.** opening of gaps in fortifications.
    ambuscadoes. ambushes. **Spanish blades.** swords
    from Toledo, where the best swords were made
44. **healths.** toasts. **five fathom deep.** a very deep or
    tall drink
45. **plats ... horses.** refers to the familiar superstition
    of "witches' stirrups," tangles in the manes of horses
46. **elflocks.** tangles thought superstitiously to be the work
    of elves, who would seek revenge if the elflocks were
    untangled
47. **learns.** teaches
48. **good carriage.** good posture
49. **vain fantasy.** empty imagination

Which is as thin of substance as the air,
And more inconstant than the wind, who woos
Even now the frozen bosom of the north,
And being angered, puffs away from thence,
Turning his side to the dew-dropping South.

BENVOLIO.
This wind you talk of blows us from ourselves. 50
Supper is done, and we shall come too late.

ROMEO.
I fear, too early; for my mind misgives 51
Some consequence yet hanging in the stars
Shall bitterly begin his fearful date 52
With this night's revels, and expire the term 53
Of a despisèd life closed in my breast
By some vile forfeit of untimely death.
But he that hath the steerage of my course
Direct my suit! On, lusty gentlemen. 54

BENVOLIO.
Strike, drum. 55

*[They march about the stage,
and retire to one side]*

---

50. from ourselves. from our plans
51. misgives. fears
52. date. appointed time
53. expire. bring to an end
54. lusty. lively
55. drum. drummer

---◆---

Synopsis of Act I, Scene 4

In Scene 4, Romeo, Benvolio, Mercutio, and several other "maskers" walked to the Capulet feast. There they planned to enter, dance once, and leave. In spite of Mercutio's clever efforts to amuse Romeo with stories of Queen Mab, Romeo still brooded about his lost love. As the scene finished, Romeo had a feeling that trouble was "hanging in the stars."

---◆---

———————◆———————

Before You Read Act I, Scene 5

In Scene 5, the two lovers meet and fall in love. Only later will they realize that as children of feuding enemies, they are in a very dangerous situation. Even at this early point in their relationship, they begin to change; Juliet growing more mature and Romeo more serious and sincere. Be aware of the great contrasts in this scene. Romeo and Juliet's moments together seem especially quiet and private because they follow the angry outburst of Tybalt and Capulet. Notice also the contrast between Romeo's description of his feelings for Juliet and what he said about his love for Rosaline in Scene 1. Shakespeare creates dramatic irony here. We know that Romeo is not scorning the Capulets, but if Tybalt had really been able to read Romeo's mind, he would have felt Romeo was doing something much worse. What mood are Romeo and Juliet in as the scene ends?

———————◆———————

ACT I. Scene 5.

Location: The action, continuous from the previous scene, is now imaginatively transferred to a hall in Capulet's house.

[SERVINGMEN *come forth with napkins*]

FIRST SERVINGMAN.
Where's Potpan, that he helps not to take away? [1]
He shift a trencher? [2] He scrape a trencher?

SECOND SERVINGMAN.
When good manners shall lie all in one or two men's
hands, and they unwashed too, tis a foul thing.

FIRST SERVINGMAN.
Away with the joint stools, [3] remove the court cupboard, [4] look to the plate. [5] Good thou, save me a
piece of marchpane, [6] and, as thou loves me, let the
porter let in Susan Grindstone and Nell.

[*Exit* SECOND SERVINGMAN]

Anthony and Potpan!

---

1. **take away.** clear the table.
2. **trencher.** wooden dish or plate
3. **joint stools.** stools with joined corners made by a
   furniture maker
4. **court cupboard.** sideboard.
5. **plate.** silverware
6. **marchpane.** cake made from sugar and almonds,
   marzipan

[Enter two more SERVINGMEN]

THIRD SERVINGMAN.
Ay, boy, ready.

FIRST SERVINGMAN.
You are looked for and called for, asked for and
sought for, in the great chamber.

FOURTH SERVINGMAN.
We cannot be here and there too. Cheerly, boys! Be
brisk awhile, and the longer liver take all. [7]

[Exit]

[Enter CAPULET *and family and all the guests
and gentlewomen to the maskers]*

CAPULET.
[To the maskers]
Welcome, gentlemen! Ladies that have their toes
Unplagued with corns will walk a bout with you. [8]
Ah, my mistresses, which of you all
Will now deny to dance? She that makes dainty, [9]
She, I'll swear, hath corns. Am I come near ye now? [10]
Welcome, gentlemen! I have seen the day
That I have worn a visor and could tell

---

7. **the longer ... all.** a proverb, "the survivor takes
   all," here used to promote seizing the moment of pleasure
8. **walk a bout.** dance a turn
9. **makes dainty.** acts coyly reluctant to dance
10. **Am ... now.** have I hit a sensitive point

A whispering tale in a fair lady's ear
Such as would please. 'Tis gone, 'tis gone, 'tis gone.
You are welcome, gentlemen! Come, musicians,
   play.

[Music plays, and they dance]

A hall, a hall! Give room! And foot it, girls. 11
[To SERVINGMEN] More light, you knaves, and
   turn the tables up, 12
And quench the fire; the room is grown too hot.
[To his cousin] Ah, sirrah, this unlooked-for sport
   comes well. 13
Nay, sit, nay, sit, good cousin Capulet, 14
For you and I are past our dancing days.
How long is 't now since last yourself and I
Were in a mask?

SECOND CAPULET.
By 'r Lady, thirty years.

CAPULET.
What, man? 'Tis not so much, 'tis not so much;
'Tis since the nuptial of Lucentio,
Come Pentecost as quickly as it will, 15
Some five-and-twenty years, and then we masked.

---

11. **A hall.** clear the hall for dancing
12. **turn the tables up.** Tables were usually made of
    hinged leaves. They were put aside for dancing.
13. **unlooked-for sport.** arrival of the maskers, making a
    dance possible
14. **cousin.** kinsman
15. **Pentecost.** seventh Sunday after Easter

SECOND CAPULET.

'Tis more, 'tis more. His son is elder, sir;
His son is thirty.

CAPULET.

Will you tell me that?
His son was but a ward two years ago. [16]

ROMEO.

[*To a* SERVINGMAN]
What lady's that which doth enrich the hand
Of yonder knight?

SERVINGMAN.

I know not, sir.

Juliet

ROMEO.

O, she doth teach the torches to burn bright!
It seems she hangs upon the cheek of night
As a rich jewel in an Ethiop's ear —
Beauty too rich for use, for earth too dear! [17]
So shows a snowy dove trooping with crows [18]
As yonder lady o'er her fellows shows.
The measure done, I'll watch her place of stand, [19]
And, touching hers, make blessèd my rude hand. [20]
Did my heart love till now? Forswear it, sight! [21]
For I ne'er saw true beauty till this night.

---

16. **a ward.** a minor under guardianship
17. **dear.** precious
18. **shows.** appears
19. **The measure done.** when this dance is over. **her place of stand.** where she stands
20. **hers.** her hand. **rude.** rough
21. **Forswear it.** deny any earlier oath

TYBALT.

This, by his voice, should be a Montague.
Fetch me my rapier, boy. What dares the slave [22]
Come hither, covered with an antic face, [23]
To fleer and scorn at our solemnity? [24]
Now, by the stock and honor of my kin,
To strike him dead I hold it not a sin.

CAPULET.

Why, how now, kinsman? Wherefore storm you so?

TYBALT.

Uncle, this is a Montague, our foe,
A villain that is hither come in spite [25]
To scorn at our solemnity this night.

CAPULET.

Young Romeo is it?

TYBALT.

'Tis he, that villain Romeo.

CAPULET.

Content thee, gentle coz, let him alone.
'A bears him like a portly gentleman, [26]
And, to say truth, Verona brags of him
To be a virtuous and well governed youth.
I would not for the wealth of all this town

---

22. **What.** how
23. **antic face.** grotesque mask
24. **fleer.** mock. **solemnity.** time-honored festivity
25. **spite.** with a grudge
26. **'A ... portly gentleman.** He behaves like a dignified
gentleman.

Here in my house do him disparagement. [27]
Therefore be patient; take no note of him.
It is my will, the which if thou respect,
Show a fair presence and put off these frowns,
An ill-beseeming semblance for a feast. [28]

TYBALT.
It fits when such a villain is a guest.
I'll not endure him.

CAPULET.
                  He shall be endured.
What, goodman boy? I say he shall. Go to! [29]
Am I the master here, or you? Go to.
You'll not endure him! God shall mend my soul,
You'll make a mutiny among my guests! [30]
You will set cock-a-hoop! You'll be the man! [31]

TYBALT.
Why, uncle, 'tis a shame.

CAPULET.
                Go to, go to,
You are a saucy boy. Is 't so, indeed?
This trick may chance to scathe you. I know what. [32]

---

27. **disparagement.** insult
28. **semblance.** facial expression
29. **goodman boy.** A belittling term; "Goodman" applied to
   one below the rank of gentleman, but still of some
   substance, like a wealthy farmer. **Go to.** an expression
   of irritation
30. **mutiny.** disturbance
31. **You ... cock-a-hoop.** You will behave recklessly, like a
   barnyard rooster. **be the man.** play the big man
32. **scathe.** harm. **what.** what I'm doing, or what I'll do

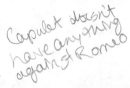
Capulet doesn't
have anything
against Romeo

You must contrary me! Marry, 'tis time. — 33
Well said, my hearts! — you are a princox, go. 34
Be quiet, or — More light, more light! — For shame!
I'll make you quiet, what! — Cheerly, my hearts!

TYBALT.

Patience perforce with willful choler meeting 35
Makes my flesh tremble in their different greeting. 36
I will withdraw. But this intrusion shall,
Now seeming sweet, convert to bitterest gall.

[Exit]

ROMEO.

[*To* JULIET]

If I profane with my unworthiest hand
  This holy shrine, the gentle sin is this: 37
My lips, two blushing pilgrims, ready stand
  To smooth that rough touch with a tender kiss.

JULIET.

Good pilgrim, you do wrong your hand too much,
  Which mannerly devotion shows in this; 38
For saints have hands that pilgrims' hands do
    touch,
  And palm to palm is holy palmers' kiss. 39

---

33. **contrary.** oppose, aggravate. **'tis time.** it's time you
   were taught a lesson
34. **Well said.** well done. **princox.** saucy boy
35. **Patience perforce.** enforced patience. **willful
   choler.** passionate anger
36. **different greeting.** antagonistic opposition
37. **shrine.** Juliet's hand
38. **mannerly.** proper
39. **palmers.** pilgrims who have been to the Holy Land and
   brought back a palm

ROMEO.
  Have not saints lips, and holy palmers too?

JULIET.
  Ay, pilgrim, lips that they must use in prayer.

ROMEO.
  kiss me
  O, then, dear saint, let lips do what hands do.
  They pray; grant thou, lest faith turn to despair. 40

JULIET.
  Saints do not move, though grant for prayers' sake. 41

ROMEO.
  Then move not, while my prayer's effect I take.
                              [*He kisses her*]

  Thus from my lips, by thine, my sin is purged.

JULIET.
  Then have my lips the sin that they have took.

ROMEO.
  Sin from my lips? O trespass sweetly urged!
  Give me my sin again.
                              [*He kisses her*]

JULIET.
                    You kiss by th' book. 42

---

40. **grant thou.** you must answer their prayers
41. **move.** take the initiative in earthly affairs. **grant.**
    they grant
42. **again.** back again. **by th' book.** by the rules, expertly

NURSE.
  [*Approaching*]
  Madam, your mother craves a word with you.

                              [JULIET *retires*]

ROMEO.
  What is her mother?

NURSE.
                              Marry, bachelor, [43]
  Her mother is the lady of the house,
  And a good lady, and a wise and virtuous.
  I nursed her daughter that you talked withal. [44]
  I tell you, he that can lay hold of her
  Shall have the chinks. [45]

ROMEO.
                              Is she a Capulet?
  O dear account! My life is my foe's debt. [46]

BENVOLIO.
  [*Approaching*]
  Away, begone! The sport is at the best. [47]

ROMEO.
  Ay, so I fear; the more is my unrest.

                    [*The maskers prepare to leave*]

---

43. **What.** who. **Marry.** by the Virgin Mary. **bachelor.**
    young man
44. **withal.** with
45. **the chinks.** plenty of money
46. **dear account.** heavy judgement. **my foe's debt.** due
    to my enemy, at his mercy
47. **The sport ... best.** it is time to go.

CAPULET.
Nay, gentlemen, prepare not to be gone.
We have a trifling foolish banquet towards. 48
[*One whispers in his ear*]
Is it e'en so? Why, then, I thank you all. 49
I thank you, honest gentlemen. Good night. 50
More torches here! Come on then, let's to bed.
[*To his cousin*] Ah, sirrah, by my fay, it waxes late. 51
I'll to my rest.

> [*All proceed to leave but
> JULIET and the NURSE*]

JULIET.
Come hither, Nurse. What is yond gentleman?

NURSE.
The son and heir of old Tiberio.

JULIET.
What's he that now is going out of door?

NURSE.
Marry, that, I think, be young Petruchio.

JULIET.
What's he that follows here, that would not dance?

NURSE.
I know not.

---

48. **foolish banquet towards.** insignificant light meal in
    preparation
49. **Is ... so?** Must you really leave?
50. **honest.** honorable
51. **fay.** faith. **waxes.** grows

JULIET.

Go ask his name. [*The* NURSE *goes*] If he be
   marrièd,
My grave is like to be my wedding bed. 52

Shall kill herself

NURSE.

[*Returning*]
His name is Romeo, and a Montague,
The only son of your great enemy.

JULIET.

My only love sprung from my only hate!
Too early seen unknown, and known too late!
Prodigious birth of love it is to me 53
That I must love a loathèd enemy.

NURSE.

What's tis? What's tis? 54

JULIET.

                        A rhyme I learned even now
Of one I danced withal.

                        [*One calls within* "Juliet"]

NURSE.

                        Anon, anon! 55
Come, let's away. The strangers all are gone.

                                          [*Exit*]

*

---

52. **like.** likely
53. **Prodigious.** ominous, dangerous
54. **tis.** this
55. **Anon.** we're coming

Synopsis of Act I, Scene 5

Capulet welcomed the maskers and encouraged them to dance. Meanwhile Capulet discussed with an elderly relative how long it had been since the two of them attended a masked ball.

During the dancing Romeo was struck by the beauty of Juliet. While he was praising Juliet's beauty, he was overheard by Tybalt, who recognized him as a Montague. The hot-tempered Tybalt would have killed Romeo then and there but old Capulet angrily stopped him. Romeo and Juliet shared in a witty, yet romantic, conversation. Soon both were in love. Only as the party ended and everyone began to leave did the two lovers learn each others identities. They were children of their fathers' hated enemies.

---◆---

Before You Read Act II, Scene 1

Act II, Scene 1 contains more irony. Mercutio and Benvolio correctly assume that Romeo is in love, but they believe the object of his affection is still Rosaline. Little do they know that his new love will create many more serious complications. Notice that Romeo's love for Juliet seems even more pure and sincere when contrasted with Mercutio's teasing comments. At the end of the scene, Romeo is left alone in Juliet's garden.

---◆---

ACT II. Scene 1.

Location: Outside of Capulet's walled orchard

[*Enter* ROMEO *alone*]

ROMEO.
Can I go forward when my heart is here? [1]
Turn back, dull earth, and find thy center out. [2]

[ROMEO *retires*]

[*Enter* BENVOLIO *with* MERCUTIO]

BENVOLIO.
Romeo! My cousin Romeo! Romeo!

MERCUTIO.
He is wise
And, on my life, hath stolen him home to bed.

BENVOLIO.
He ran this way and leapt this orchard wall.
Call, good Mercutio.

MERCUTIO.
Nay, I'll conjure too. [3]
Romeo! Humors! Madman! Passion! Lover! [4]
Appear thou in the likeness of a sigh.
Speak but one rhyme, and I am satisfied!
Cry but "Ay me!" Pronounce but "love" and "dove."
Speak to my gossip Venus one fair word, [5]

---

1. **forward.** away
2. **dull earth.** lifeless body.   **center.** Juliet
3. **conjure.** say a spell that will bring Romeo
4. **Humors.** moods
5. **gossip.** crony, merry old lady

One nickname for her purblind son and heir, [6]
Young Abraham Cupid, he that shot so trim [7]
When King Cophetua loved the beggar maid. — [8]
He heareth not, he stirreth not, he moveth not;
The ape is dead, and I must conjure him. — [9]
I conjure thee by Rosaline's bright eyes,
By her high forehead and her scarlet lip,
*
That in thy likeness thou appear to us!

BENVOLIO.
An if he hear thee, thou wilt anger him. [10]

MERCUTIO.
This cannot anger him. 'Twould anger him
To raise a spirit in his mistress' circle [11]
Of some strange nature, letting it there stand [12]
Till she had laid it and conjured it down; [13]
That were some spite. My invocation [14]
Is fair and honest; in his mistress' name
I conjure only but to raise up him.

---

6. **purblind.** dim-sighted
7. **Young Abraham.** one who is young and yet old, like the Biblical Abraham; Cupid was the youngest and oldest of the gods
8. **King Cophetua.** In an old song, the King falls in love with a beggar girl and makes her his queen.
9. **ape.** a term of endearment
10. **An if.** if
11. **circle.** conjuring circle
12. **strange.** belonging to another person
13. **laid it.** laid the spirit to rest
14. **were.** would be. **spite.** injury, vexation

BENVOLIO.
Come, he hath hid himself among these trees
To be consorted with the humorous night. [15]
Blind is his love, and best befits the dark.

MERCUTIO.
If love be blind, love cannot hit the mark.
*
Romeo, good night. I'll to my truckle bed; [16]
This field bed is too cold for me to sleep.
Come, shall we go?

BENVOLIO.
                    Go, then for 'tis in vain
To seek him here that means not to be found.

[*Exit with* MERCUTIO]

---

15. **consorted.** associated.   **humorous.** moist; also,
    influenced by humor or mood
16. **truckle bed.** a bed on casters that rolls under a
    standing bed

------------------◆------------------

Synopsis of Act II, Scene 1

After the masked ball, Romeo jumped over the wall into Capulet's orchard, where he hoped to catch another glimpse of Juliet. His friends looked for him there. Mercutio teased him about Rosaline. Benvolio just called to him. However, Romeo remained hidden. Benvolio, knowing that Romeo liked to be alone, persuaded Mercutio to leave.

------------------◆------------------

———————◆———————

Before You Read Act II, Scene 2

Scene 2 is one of the poetic and romantic high points of *Romeo and Juliet*. Notice how this scene emphasizes the haste and recklessness of the courtship and hints at the coming tragedy. In spite of the romantic mood, the lovers feel flashes of fear at the danger in their relationship; Juliet knows that their love is "too rash, too unadvised, too sudden." Yet through it all, notice how the two lovers grow and change. How are the two lovers different in this scene?

———————◆———————

ACT II. Scene 2.

Location: The action, continuous from the previous scene, is now imaginatively transferred to inside Capulet's orchard. A rhymed couplet links the two scenes. Romeo has been hiding from his friends as though concealed by the orchard wall. He speaks at once, then turns to observe Juliet's window, which is probably in the gallery above, rearstage.

ROMEO.
  [*Coming forward*]
  He jests at scars that never felt a wound.

  [*A light appears above, as at* JULIET'S *window*]

  But soft, what light through yonder window breaks?
  It is the east, and Juliet is the sun.   dark → light
  Arise, fair sun, and kill the envious moon,
  Who is already sick and pale with grief
  That thou her maid art far more fair than she. [1]
  Be not her maid, since she is envious;
  Her vestal livery is but sick and green [2]
  And none but fools do wear it. Cast it off.

          [JULIET *is visible at her window*]

  It is my lady, O, it is my love!
  O, that she knew she were!
  She speaks, yet she says nothing. What of that?

---

1. **maid.** worshipper of Diana, goddess of the moon and patroness of virgins
2. **Her vestal livery.** the uniform of Diana's chaste followers

Her eye discourses; I will answer it.
I am too bold. 'Tis not to me she speaks.
Two of the fairest stars in all the heaven,
Having some business, do entreat her eyes
To twinkle in their spheres till they return. [3]
What if her eyes were there, they in her head?
The brightness of her cheek would shame those stars
As daylight doth a lamp; her eyes in heaven
Would through the airy region stream so bright [4]
That birds would sing and think it were not night.
See how she leans her cheek upon her hand!
O, that I were a glove upon that hand,
That I might touch that cheek!

JULIET.

Ay me!

ROMEO.

She speaks!
O, speak again, bright angel, for thou art
As glorious to this night, being o'er my head,
As is a winged messenger of heaven
Unto the white-upturnèd wondering eyes [5]
Of mortals that fall back to gaze on him
When he bestrides the lazy puffing clouds
And sails upon the bosom of the air.

JULIET.
O Romeo, Romeo, wherefore art thou Romeo? [6]
Deny thy father and refuse thy name!

---

3. **spheres.** orbits
4. **stream.** shine
5. **white-upturnèd.** looking upward so that the whites of
   the eyes can be seen
6. **wherefore.** why

Or, if thou wilt not, be but sworn my love,
And I'll no longer be a Capulet.

ROMEO.
[*Aside*]
Shall I hear more, or shall I speak at this?

JULIET.
'Tis but thy name that is my enemy;
Thou art thyself, though not a Montague. [7]
What's Montague? It is nor hand, nor foot, [8]
Nor arm, nor face, nor any other part
Belonging to a man. O, be some other name!
What's in a name? That which we call a rose
By any other word would smell as sweet;
So Romeo would, were he not Romeo called,
Retain that dear perfection which he owes [9]
Without that title. Romeo, doff thy name, [10]
And for thy name, which is no part of thee, [11]
Take all myself.

ROMEO.
              I take thee at thy word!
Call me but love, and I'll be new baptized;
Henceforth I never will be Romeo.

JULIET.
What man art thou that, thus bescreened in night, [12]

---

7. **though not a Montague.** i.e., even if you were not a
   Montague
8. **nor hand.** neither hand
9. **owes.** possesses, owns
10. **doff.** cast off, remove
11. **for.** in exchange for
12. **bescreened.** concealed, hidden

So stumblest on my counsel? [13]

ROMEO.

By a name
I know not how to tell thee who I am.
My name, dear saint, is hateful to myself,
Because it is an enemy to thee;
Had I it written, I would tear the word.

JULIET.
My ears have not yet drunk a hundred words
Of thy tongue's uttering, yet I know the sound:
Art thou not Romeo and a Montague?

ROMEO.
Neither, fair maid, if either thee dislike. [14]

JULIET.
How camest thou hither, tell me, and wherefore?
The orchard walls are high and hard to climb,
And the place death, considering who thou art,
If any of my kinsmen find thee here.

ROMEO.
With love's light wings did I o'erperch these walls, [15]
For stony limits cannot hold love out,
And what love can do, that dares love attempt;
Therefore thy kinsmen are no stop to me.

JULIET.
If they do see thee, they will murder thee.

worries about him

---

13. **counsel.** secret thought
14. **thee dislike.** displease you
15. **o'erperch.** fly over

ROMEO.
Alack, there lies more peril in thine eye
Than twenty of their swords. Look thou but sweet,
And I am proof against their enmity. [16]

JULIET.
I would not for the world they saw thee here.

ROMEO. *I'd rather die now loving you*
I have night's cloak to hide me from their eyes;
And but thou love me, let them find me here. [17] *desperate*
My life were better ended by their hate
Than death proroguèd, wanting of thy love. [18]

JULIET.
By whose direction foundst thou out this place?

ROMEO.
By love, that first did prompt me to inquire.
He lent me counsel, and I lent him eyes.
I am no pilot; yet, wert thou as far
As that vast shore washed with the farthest sea,
I should adventure for such merchandise. [19]

JULIET.
Thou knowest the mask of night is on my face,
Else would a maiden blush bepaint my cheek
For that which thou hast heard me speak tonight.
Fain would I dwell on form — fain, fain deny [20]

---

16. **proof.** shielded, protected
17. **but.** unless
18. **proroguèd.** postponed. **wanting of.** lacking
19. **adventure.** risk or long journey
20. **Fain.** gladly. **dwell on form.** follow the proper way to
    behave, etiquette

What I have spoke; but farewell compliment! [21]
Dost thou love me? I know thou wilt say "Ay,"
And I will take thy word. Yet if thou swear'st
Thou mayst prove false. At lovers' perjuries,
They say, Jove laughs. O gentle Romeo,
If thou dost love, pronounce it faithfully.
Or if thou thinkest I am too quickly won,
I'll frown and be perverse and say thee nay, [22]
So thou wilt woo, but else not for the world. [23]
In truth, fair Montague, I am too fond, [24]
And therefore thou mayst think my havior light. [25]
But trust me, gentleman, I'll prove more true
Than those that have more coying to be strange. [26]
I should have been more strange, I must confess,
But that thou overheardst, ere I was ware, [27]
My true-love passion. Therefore pardon me,
And not impute this yielding to light love,
Which the dark night hath so discoverèd. [28]

ROMEO.
Lady, by yonder blessèd moon I vow,
That tips with silver all these fruit-tree tops —

JULIET.
O, swear not by the moon, th' inconstant moon,

---

21. **compliment.** conventional behavior, etiquette
22. **be perverse.** act oppositely to true feelings
23. **So.** as long as, if only. **else.** otherwise
24. **fond.** infatuated
25. **havior light.** behavior frivolous or silly
26. **coying.** coyness, cunning. **strange.** reserved, aloof, modest
27. **ware.** aware
28. **which.** which yielding. **discoverèd.** revealed

That monthly changes in her circled orb, [29]
Lest that thy <u>love prove likewise variable.</u>

ROMEO.
What shall I swear by?

JULIET.
                                Do not swear at all;
Or, if thou wilt, swear by thy gracious self,
Which is the god of my idolatry,
And I'll believe thee.

ROMEO.
                          If my heart's dear love —

JULIET.
Well, do not swear. Although I joy in thee,
I have no joy of this contract tonight. [30]
It is too rash, too unadvised, too sudden, [31]
Too like the lightning, which doth cease to be
Ere one can say "It lightens." Sweet, good night!
This bud of love, by summer's ripening breath,
May prove a beauteous flower when next we meet.
Good night, good night ! As sweet repose and rest [32]
Come to thy heart as that within my breast!

Doesn't want to rush things

ROMEO.
O, wilt thou leave me so unsatisfied?

---

29. orb. sphere, orbit
30. contract. exchanging of vows
31. unadvised. unconsidered
32. As. may just as

JULIET.
What satisfaction canst thou have tonight?

ROMEO.
Th' exchange of thy love's faithful vow for mine.

JULIET.
I gave thee mine before thou didst request it;
And yet I would it were to give again. ³³

ROMEO.
Wouldst thou withdraw it? For what purpose, love?

JULIET.
But to be frank and give it thee again. ³⁴
And yet I wish but for the thing I have.
My bounty is as boundless as the sea, ³⁵
My love as deep; the more I give to thee,
The more I have, for both are infinite.
                    [*The* NURSE *calls within*]
I hear some noise within; dear love, adieu! —
Anon, good Nurse! — Sweet Montague, be true.
Stay but a little, I will come again.
                              [*Exit, above*]

ROMEO.
O blessèd, blessèd night! I am afeard,
Being in night, all this is but a dream,
Too flattering-sweet to be substantial. ³⁶

---

33. were. were available
34. frank. generous
35. bounty. what I have to give
36. substantial. real

[*Enter* JULIET, *above*]

Mother

JULIET.
Three words, dear Romeo, and good night indeed.
If that thy bent of love be honorable, [37]
Thy purpose marriage, send me word tomorrow,
By one that I'll procure to come to thee,
Where and what time thou wilt perform the rite;
And all my fortunes at thy foot I'll lay
And follow thee my lord throughout the world.

NURSE.
[*Within*] Madam!

JULIET.
I come, anon. — But if thou meanest not well,
I do beseech thee —

NURSE.
[*Within*] Madam!

JULIET.
By and by, I come — [38]
To cease thy strife and leave me to my grief. [39]
Tomorrow will I send.

ROMEO.
So thrive my soul —

JULIET.
A thousand times good night!

[*Exit, above*]

---

37. bent. purpose
38. By and by. immediately
39. strife. efforts

ROMEO.

A thousand times the worse, to want thy light.
Love goes toward love as schoolboys from their books,
But love from love, toward school with heavy looks.

[He starts to leave]

[Enter JULIET above, again]

JULIET.

Hist! Romeo, hist! O, for a falconer's voice,
To lure this tassel-gentle back again! [40]
Bondage is hoarse and may not speak aloud, [41]
Else would I tear the cave where Echo lies [42]
And make her airy tongue more hoarse than mine
With repetition of "My Romeo!"

ROMEO.

It is my soul that calls upon my name.
How silver-sweet sound lovers' tongues by night,
Like softest music to attending ears!

JULIET.
Romeo!

ROMEO.

My nyas? [43]

---

40. tassel-gentle. the male of the goshawk
41. Bondage is hoarse. in confinement caused by family
restrictions, one can speak only in a loud whisper
42. tear. pierce with noise. **Echo.** In mythology Echo,
rejected by Narcissus, pines away in lonely caves until
only her voice is left.
43. nyas. eyas, fledgling or young bird

JULIET.

> What o'clock tomorrow
> Shall I send to thee?

ROMEO.

> By the hour of nine.

JULIET.

> I will not fail. 'Tis twenty years till then. —
> I have forgot why I did call thee back.

ROMEO.

> Let me stand here till thou remember it.

JULIET.

> I shall forget, to have thee still stand there, [44]
> Remembering how I love thy company.

ROMEO.

> And I'll still stay, to have thee still forget,
> Forgetting any other home but this.

JULIET.

> 'Tis almost morning. I would have thee gone —
> And yet no farther than a wanton's bird, [45]
> That lets it hop a little from his hand,
> Like a poor prisoner in his twisted gyves, [46]
> And with a silken thread plucks it back again,
> So loving-jealous of his liberty. [47]

---

44. **still.** always
45. **wanton's.** spoiled child's
46. **gyves.** chains
47. **his.** its

ROMEO.
I would I were thy bird.

JULIET.
> Sweet, so would I.
Yet I should kill thee with much cherishing.
Good night, good night! Parting is such sweet *paradox*
sorrow
That I shall say good night till it be morrow.

> [*Exit, above*]

ROMEO.
Sleep dwell upon thine eyes, peace in thy breast!
Would I were sleep and peace, so sweet to rest!
Hence will I to my ghostly friar's close cell, [48]
His help to crave, and my dear hap to tell. [49]

> [*Exit*]

---

48. ghostly. spiritual.   **close.** small
49. dear hap. good fortune

———————◆———————

Synopsis of Act II, Scene 2

In Scene 2, Romeo remained in the orchard, thinking about his new love. Soon, Juliet appeared in her chamber window. In a soliloquy, Romeo compared Juliet to the sun. Thinking that she was alone, Juliet revealed her love for Romeo as she began "O Romeo, Romeo! Wherefore art thou Romeo?" He then spoke to her and expressed his love for her. They agreed to marry, in spite of the complications both recognize. Twice the Nurse called Juliet to bed, but twice she returned for another word with Romeo. As day broke, the lovers finally said farewell.

———————◆———————

------------◆------------

Before You Read Act II, Scene 3

In this scene, notice that where Romeo is eager, even impatient, the Friar is philosophical and thorough. The Friar suggests that caution and well-thought-out affection are a wiser course. Notice also that the Friar is an expert on herbs and medicines. Consider why Shakespeare stressed this special talent. The Friar knows the good and evil potions can do. In talking about this, he reminds us of the good and evil that are a part of making this tragedy. In spite of his worries about the marriage, he realizes that it could end the feud between the Montagues and the Capulets. Why might Friar Laurence think that?

------------◆------------

ACT II. Scene 3.

Location: Verona. Near Friar Laurence's cell, perhaps in the monastery garden.

[*Enter* FRIAR LAURENCE *alone, with a basket*]

FRIAR LAURENCE.
The gray-eyed morn smiles on the frowning night,
Check'ring the eastern clouds with streaks of light,
And fleckled darkness like a drunkard reels [1]
From forth day's path and Titan's fiery wheels. [2]
Now, ere the sun advance his burning eye, [3]
The day to cheer and night's dank dew to dry,
I must up-fill this osier cage of ours [4]
With baleful weeds and precious-juicèd flowers. [5]
The earth that's nature's mother is her tomb;
What is her burying grave, that is her womb;
And from her womb children of divers kind [6]
We sucking on her natural bosom find,
Many for many virtues excellent,
None but for some, and yet all different. [7]
O, mickle is the powerful grace that lies [8]
In plants, herbs, stones, and their true qualities. [9]

---

1. **fleckled.** spotted
2. **From forth.** out of the way of. **Titan's.** Helios, the sun god, a titan
3. **advance.** raise
4. **osier cage.** willow basket
5. **baleful.** harmful
6. **divers.** different
7. **None but for some.** there are none that are not useful for something
8. **mickle.** great. **grace.** heavenly power
9. **true.** proper, inherent

Nothing so bad it can't be good – vice versa

{ For naught so vile that on the earth doth live [10]
{ But to the earth some special good doth give;
{ Nor aught so good but, strained from that fair use, [11]
{ Revolts from true birth, stumbling on abuse. [12]
Virtue itself turns vice, being misapplied,
And vice sometime's by action dignified.

too much of a good thing

good meaning bad outcome

[*Enter* ROMEO]

Within the infant rind of this weak flower [13] *relationship*
Poison hath residence and medicine power:
For this, being smelt, with that part cheers each
    part; [14]
Being tasted, stays all senses with the heart. [15]
Two such opposèd kings encamp them still [16]
In man as well as herbs — grace and rude will;
And where the worser is predominant,
Full soon the canker death eats up that plant. [17]

Foxglove

ROMEO. *– weak flower (bud) → depression*
Good morrow, Father.

FRIAR LAURENCE.
                Benedicite! [18]
What early tongue so sweet saluteth me?

---

10. **For naught so vile.** for there is nothing so vile
11. **strained.** forced, perverted
12. **Revolts ... birth.** conflicts with its true purpose
13. **infant rind.** tender skin
14. **that part.** i.e., the odor
15. **stays.** halts
16. **still.** always
17. **canker.** cankerworm, a destructive caterpillar
18. **Benedicite.** a blessing on you

He can tell us something up.

Young son, it argues a distempered head [19]
So soon to bid good morrow to thy bed.
Care keeps his watch in every old man's eye,
And where care lodges sleep will never lie;
But where unbruisèd youth with unstuffed brain [20]
Doth couch his limbs, there golden sleep doth reign.
Therefore thy earliness doth me assure
Thou art uproused with some distemp'rature; [21]
Or if not so, then here I hit it right:
Our Romeo hath not been in bed tonight.

ROMEO.
That last is true. The sweeter rest was mine.

FRIAR LAURENCE. *knows Romeo well*
God pardon sin! Wast thou with Rosaline?

ROMEO.
With Rosaline, my ghostly father? No.
I have forgot that name, and that name's woe.

FRIAR LAURENCE.
That's my good son. But where hast thou been, then?

ROMEO.
I'll tell thee ere thou ask it me again.
I have been feasting with mine enemy,
Where on a sudden one hath wounded me
That's by me wounded. Both our remedies [22]

---

19. **argues** demonstrates, provides evidence of.
    distempered. troubled
20. **unstuffed.** not overcharged, carefree
21. **distemp'rature.** illness
22. **Both our remedies.** i.e., the cure for both of us

you can help me

Within thy help and holy physic lies. [23]
I bear no hatred, blessèd man, for, lo,
My intercession likewise steads my foe. [24]

FRIAR LAURENCE.

Be plain, good son, and homely in thy drift. [25]
Riddling confession finds but riddling shrift. [26]

ROMEO.

Then plainly know my heart's dear love is set
On the fair daughter of rich Capulet.
As mine on hers, so hers is set on mine,
And all combined, save what thou must combine [27]
By holy marriage. When and where and how
We met, we wooed, and made exchange of vow
I'll tell thee as we pass; but this I pray,
That thou consent to marry us today.

FRIAR LAURENCE.

Holy Saint Francis, what a change is here!
Is Rosaline, that thou didst love so dear,
So soon forsaken? Young men's love then lies
Not truly in their hearts, but in their eyes.
Jesu Maria, what a deal of brine [28]
Hath washed thy sallow cheeks for Rosaline! [29]
How much salt water thrown away in waste
To season love, that of it doth not taste!

*He's throwing love
around like it's
nothing*

---

23. **physic.** medicine
24. **intercession.** petition. **steads.** helps
25. **homely.** simple. **drift.** speech
26. **shrift.** absolution, confession
27. **save.** except
28. **brine.** salt water; tears
29. **sallow.** sickly yellow

The sun not yet thy sighs from heaven clears,
Thy old groans yet ringing in mine ancient ears.
Lo, here upon thy cheek the stain doth sit
Of an old tear that is not washed off yet.
If e'er thou wast thyself and these woes thine, [30]
Thou and these woes were all for Rosaline.
And art thou changed? Pronounce this sentence
    then: [31]
Women may fall, when there's no strength in men. [32]

ROMEO.
Thou chidst me oft for loving Rosaline. [33]

FRIAR LAURENCE.
For doting, not for loving, pupil mine. [34]

ROMEO.
And badst me bury love. [35]

FRIAR LAURENCE.
               Not in a grave
To lay one in, another out to have.

ROMEO.
I pray thee, chide not. She whom I love now
Doth grace for grace and love for love allow. [36]
The other did not so.

---

30. wast thyself. were sincere
31. sentence. conclusion, judgement
32. fall. be weak.   **strength.** constancy, stability
33. chidst. scolded
34. doting. being infatuated
35. badst. bade, asked
36. grace. favor, graciousness.   **allow.** give

FRIAR LAURENCE.
O, she knew well
Thy love did read by rote, that could not spell. [37]
But come, young waverer, come, go with me.
In one respect I'll thy assistant be; [38]
For this alliance may so happy prove
To turn your households' rancor to pure love. [39]

Bring households to peace

Doesn't question himself

ROMEO.
O, let us hence! I stand on sudden haste. [40]

FRIAR LAURENCE.
Wisely and slow. They stumble that run fast.

foreshadowing?

[Exit]

---

37. **did read by rote.** repeated words from memory without
    understanding them
38. **In one respect.** for one reason (at least)
39. **To.** as to. **rancor.** hatred
40. **stand on.** am in need of, insist on

---◆---

Synopsis of Act II, Scene 3

Friar Laurence, Romeo's friend and confessor, was up early to gather herbs. He spoke about the fact that some plants can be good and evil, medicines and poisons. He extended this idea of good and evil to man. Romeo Montague arrived and told the Friar of the love that had developed between Juliet Capulet and himself. Romeo then asked the Friar to marry them. After gently scolding Romeo for forgetting Rosaline so quickly, the Friar agreed to Romeo's request. Friar Laurence hoped that the marriage would end the feud between the lovers' families.

---◆---

Before You Read Act II, Scene 4

Suspense begins to build in Scene 4 when we learn that Tybalt has challenged Romeo to a duel, combat between two people using swords. Notice how Tybalt's nasty temper is stressed. There is new evidence of Mercutio's hatred of Tybalt. The theme of duelling is repeated in a lighter vein in the duel of wits between Romeo and Mercutio. The idea of dueling repeats for a third time in the silly battle between the Nurse and Mercutio. Think of why this comedy is especially effective in this scene. The speed of the courtship is once again emphasized. Also notice the atmosphere of happy anticipation that is created.

ACT II. Scene 4.

Location: Verona. A street.

[*Enter* BENVOLIO *and* MERCUTIO]

MERCUTIO.
Where the devil should this Romeo be? [1]
Came he not home tonight? [2]

BENVOLIO.
Not to his father's. I spoke with his man.

MERCUTIO. oblivious to Juliet
Why, that same pale hardhearted wench, that
    Rosaline,
Torments him so that he will sure run mad.

BENVOLIO.
Tybalt, the kinsman to old Capulet,
Hath sent a letter to his father's house.

MERCUTIO.
A challenge, on my life.

BENVOLIO.
Romeo will answer it. [3] punny

MERCUTIO.
Any man that can write may answer a letter.

---

1. **should.** can
2. **tonight.** last night
3. **answer it.** accept the challenge

BENVOLIO.

Nay, he will answer the letter's master, how he dares, being dared.

MERCUTIO.

Alas poor Romeo! He is already dead, stabbed with a white wench's black eye, run through the ear with a love song, the very pin [4] of his heart cleft with the blind bow-boy's butt shaft. [5] And is he a man to encounter Tybalt?

BENVOLIO.

Why, what is Tybalt?

MERCUTIO.

More than prince of cats. [6] O, he's the courageous captain of compliments. [7] He fights as you sing prick song, [8] keeps time, distance, and proportion; he rests his minim [9] rests, one, two, and the third in your bosom. The very butcher of a silk button, [10] a duellist, a duellist, a gentleman of the very first

---

4. **pin.** peg in the center of a target. **cleft.** pierced
5. **butt shaft.** unbarbed arrow, allotted to children and to Cupid
6. **prince of cats.** The name of the king of cats in the medieval stories of Reynard the Fox was Tybalt or Tybert.
7. **captain of compliments.** master of ceremony and dueling etiquette
8. **prick song.** music written out **proportion.** rhythm
9. **minim rests.** short rests in musical notation
10. **butcher ... button.** a fencer who can hit a specific button on his adversary's person

house, [11] of the first and second cause. [12] Ah, the immortal *passado*! [13] The *punto reverso*! The *hay*!

BENVOLIO.
The what? *-doesn't fight*

MERCUTIO.
The pox of such antic, [14] lisping, affecting phantasimes, these new tuners of accent! [15] "By Jesu, a very good blade! A very tall man!" [16] *Why, is not this a lamentable thing, grandsire, [17] that we should be thus afflicted with these strange flies, [18] these fashionmongers, these pardon-me's, [19] who stand so much on the new form that they cannot sit at ease on the old bench? [20] O, their bones, their bones! [21]   *pun*

hates French

---

11. **first house.** best school of fencing
12. **first and second cause.** reasons according to the code of dueling that would cause a gentleman to challenge another
13. *passado*. forward thrust. *punto reverso*. backhanded stroke. *hay*. thrust through
14. **The pox of.** plague take. **antic.** grotesque **phantasimes.** absurd characters
15. **new tuners of accent.** those who speak in new foreign words and weird slang phrases
16. **tall.** valiant
17. **grandsire.** one who disapproves the new fashion and prefers old custom
18. **flies.** parasites
19. **pardon-me's.** people who have ridiculous, overly polite manners. **stand.** insist
20. **bench.** meaning both "fashion" or "code of manners" and "bench."
21. **bones.** French *bon*, good

motif - people not knowing what they need to know / people thinking they know

[*Enter* ROMEO]

BENVOLIO.
Here comes Romeo, here comes Romeo.

MERCUTIO.
Without his roe, [22] like a dried herring. O flesh, flesh, how art thou fishified! Now is he for the numbers that Petrarch flowed in. [23] Laura to his lady was but a kitchen wench-marry, she had a better love to berhyme her-Dido a dowdy [24], Cleopatra a gypsy, Helen and Hero hildings [25] and harlots, Thisbe a gray eye or so, but not [26] to the purpose. Signor Romeo, *bonjour*! There's a French salutation to your French slop. [27] You gave us the counterfeit fairly [28] last night.

ROMEO.
Good morrow to you both. What counterfeit did I give you?

MERCUTIO. *pun*
The slip, sir, the slip. Can you not conceive? [29]

---

22. **without his roe.** looking thin and emaciated, worn out
23. **numbers.** verses. **Laura.** the lady to whom the Italian Renaissance poet Petrarch addressed his love poems. The other romantic heroines named in the passage are also important figures in European love literature. **to.** in comparison to
24. **dowdy.** homely woman. **gypsy.** Egyptian
25. **hildings.** good-for-nothings
26. **not.** that is not
27. **French slop.** loose trousers of French fashion
28. **fairly.** handsomely, effectively
29. **slip.** counterfeit coins. **conceive.** get the joke

ROMEO.
Pardon, good Mercutio, my business was great,and
in such a case [30] as mine a man may strain courtesy.

MERCUTIO.
That's as much as to say, such a case as yours
constrains a man to bow in the hams. [31]

ROMEO.
Meaning, to curtsy. [32]

MERCUTIO.
Thou hast most kindly hit it. [33]

ROMEO.
A most courteous exposition.

MERCUTIO.
Nay, I am the very pink of courtesy.

ROMEO.
Pink for flower.

MERCUTIO.
Right.

ROMEO.
Why then is my pump well flowered. [34]

---

30. case. situation
31. bow in the hams. kneel, curtsy
32. curtsy. make obeisance
33. kindly. naturally; politely
34. pump. shoe. **well flowered.** expertly pinked or
perforated in ornamental figures

MERCUTIO.

Sure wit, follow me this jest now till thou hast worn out thy pump, that when the single sole of it is worn, the jest may remain, after the wearing, solely singular. [35]

ROMEO.

O single-soled jest, solely singular for the singleness! [36]

MERCUTIO.

Come between us, good Benvolio. My wits faints.

ROMEO.

Switch and spurs, switch and spurs! [37] Or I'll cry a match.

MERCUTIO.

Nay, if our wits run the wild-goose chase, [38] I am done, for thou hast more of the wild goose in one of thy wits than, I am sure, I have in my whole five. Was I with you there for the goose? [39]

ROMEO.

Thou wast never with me for anything when thou wast not there for the goose. [40]

---

35. **solely singular.** unique
36. **single-soled.** thin, contemptible.   **singleness.** weakness
37. **Switch and spurs.** keep up the quick pace in the game of wits.   **cry a match.** claim victory
38. **wild-goose chase.** a horse race in which the leading rider dares his competitors to follow him wherever he goes
39. **Was ... goose.** did I score a point by calling you a goose
40. **for the goose.** behaving like a goose

MERCUTIO.
I will bite thee by the ear for that jest.

ROMEO.
Nay, good goose, bite not.

MERCUTIO. *compared to a goose - loud, annoying, guard geese don't let you*
Thy wit is a very bitter sweeting, [41] it is a most get
sharp sauce. [42] *away with anything*

ROMEO.
And is it not, then, well served in to a sweet goose?

MERCUTIO.
O, here's a wit of cheveril, [43] that stretches from an
inch narrow to an ell [44] broad!

ROMEO.
I stretch it out for that word "broad," [45] which,
added to the goose, proves thee far and wide a broad
goose.

MERCUTIO.
Why, is not this better now than groaning for love?
Now art thou sociable, now art thou Romeo; now art
thou what thou art, by art as well as by nature. For
this driveling love is like a great natural [46] that

Romeo's back

---

41. **sweeting.** sweet-flavored variety of apple
42. **sharp sauce.** "biting" retort; tart sauce that should be
    served with goose
43. **cheveril.** kid leather, easily stretched
44. **ell.** forty-five inches
45. **broad.** large, complete
46. **natural.** idiot

runs lolling [47] up and down to hide his bauble in a hole.

BENVOLIO.
Stop there, stop there.

MERCUTIO.
Thou desirest me to stop in my tale against the hair. [48]

BENVOLIO.
Thou wouldst else have made thy tale large.

MERCUTIO.
O, thou art deceived; I would have made it short, for I was come to the whole depth of my tale and meant indeed to occupy the argument no longer. [49]

ROMEO.
Here's goodly gear! [50]

[*Enter* NURSE *and her man* PETER]

A sail, a sail!

MERCUTIO.
Two, two: a shirt and a smock. [51]

NURSE.
Peter!

---

47. lolling. with his tongue hanging out.   **bauble.** toy
48. against the hair. against the grain, against my wish
49. occupy the argument. talk about the matter
50. gear. substance, stuff
51. a shirt ... smock. i.e., a man and a woman

PETER.
 Anon!

NURSE.
 My fan, Peter.

MERCUTIO.
 Good Peter, to hide her face, for her fan's the fairer
 face.

NURSE.
 God gi' good morrow, gentlemen.

MERCUTIO.
 God gi' good e'en, fair gentlewoman.

NURSE.
 Is it good e'en? [52]

MERCUTIO.
 'Tis no less, I tell ye.*

NURSE.
 Out upon you! What a man are you? [53]

ROMEO.
 One, gentlewoman, that God hath made for himself
 to mar. [54]

NURSE.
 By my troth, [55] it is well said. "For himself to mar,"

---

52. **Is it good e'en.** is it afternoon already
53. **Out upon you.** expression of indignation
54. **mar.** disfigure morally through sin
55. **troth.** faith

quoth 'a? [56] Gentlemen, can any of you tell me where
I may find the young Romeo?

ROMEO.

I can tell you; but young Romeo will be older when
you have found him than he was when you sought
him. I am the youngest of that name, for fault [57] of a
worse.   *Marriage.*

NURSE.

You say well.

MERCUTIO.

Yea, is the worst well? Very well took, [58] i' faith,
wisely, wisely.

NURSE.

If you be he, sir, I desire some confidence with you. [59]
*

MERCUTIO.

Romeo, will you come to your father's? We'll to
dinner thither.

ROMEO.

I will follow you.

MERCUTIO.

Farewell, ancient lady. Farewell, [*Singing*] "Lady,
lady, lady." [60]

[*Exit* MERCUTIO *and* BENVOLIO]

---

56. quoth 'a. said he
57. fault. lack
58. took. understood
59. confidence. The Nurse means conference.
60. "Lady, lady, lady". a line from the ballad *Chaste Susanna*

NURSE.

I pray you, sir, what saucy merchant [61] was this
that was so full of his ropery? [62]

ROMEO.

A gentleman, Nurse, that loves to hear himself talk,
and will speak more in a minute than he will stand
to [63] in a month.

NURSE.

An 'a speak anything against me, I'll take him
down, [64] an 'a were lustier than he is, and twenty
such Jacks; [65] and if I cannot, I'll find those that
shall. Scurvy knave! I am none of his flirt-gills. [66] I
am none of his skains-mates. [67] [*To* PETER] And
thou must stand by, too, and suffer every knave to
use me at his pleasure!

PETER.

I saw no man use you at his pleasure. If I had, my
weapon should quickly have been out; I warrant
you, I dare draw as soon as another man, if I see
occasion in a good quarrel, and the law on my side.

---

61. **merchant.** fellow
62. **ropery.** The Nurse means roguery, or the conduct of a
    rogue.
63. **stand to.** perform, abide by
64. **take him down.** cut him down to size
65. **Jacks.** used as a term of contempt
66. **flirt-gills.** loose women
67. **skains-mates.** outlaws, criminals

NURSE.

Now, afore God, I am so vexed that every part about me quivers. Scurvy knave! Pray you, sir, a word; and as I told you, my young lady bid me inquire you out. What she bid me say, I will keep to myself. But first let me tell ye, if ye should lead her in a fool's paradise, as they say, it were a very gross kind of behavior, as they say. For the gentlewoman is young; and therefore if you should deal double with her, truly it were an ill thing to be offered to any gentlewoman, and very weak [68] dealing.

ROMEO.

Nurse, commend [69] me to thy lady and mistress. I protest [70] unto thee —

NURSE.

Good heart, and i' faith I will tell her as much. Lord, Lord, she will be a joyful woman.

ROMEO.

What wilt thou tell her, Nurse? Thou dost not mark me. [71]

NURSE.

I will tell her, sir, that you do protest, which, as I take it, is a gentlemanlike offer.

---

68. **weak.** contemptible
69. **commend me.** convey my respect and best wishes
70. **protest.** vow
71. **mark.** attend to, listen to

ROMEO.
Bid her devise
Some means to come to shrift this afternoon, [72]
And there she shall at Friar Laurence' cell
Be shrived and married. Here is for thy pains. [73]

[*He offers money*]

NURSE.
No, truly, sir, not a penny.

ROMEO.
Go to, I say you shall.

NURSE.
This afternoon, sir? Well, she shall be there.

ROMEO.
And stay, good Nurse, behind the abbey wall.
Within this hour my man shall be with thee
And bring thee cords made like a tackled stair, [74]
Which to the high topgallant of my joy [75]
Must be my convoy in the secret night. [76]
Farewell. Be trusty, and I'll quit thy pains. [77]
Farewell. Commend me to thy mistress.

[ROMEO *starts to leave*]

NURSE.
Now God in heaven bless thee! Hark you, sir.

---

72. shrift. confession and absolution
73. shrived. absolved
74. tackled stair. rope ladder
75. topgallant. highest mast and sail of a ship, the summit
76. convoy. conveyance, means of passage
77. quit. reward, pay you back for

ROMEO.

What sayst thou, my dear Nurse?

NURSE.

Is your man secret? Did you ne'er hear say, [78]
"Two may keep counsel, putting one away"? [79]

ROMEO.

'Warrant thee, my man's as true as steel.

NURSE.

Well, sir, my mistress is the sweetest lady — Lord,
Lord! When 'twas a little prating [80] thing — O,
there is a nobleman in town, one Paris, that would
fain [81] lay knife aboard; but she, good soul, had as
lief see a toad, a very toad, as see him. I anger her
sometimes and tell her that Paris is the properer [82]
man, but I'll warrant you, when I say so, she looks
as pale as any clout [83] in the versal world. Doth
not rosemary and Romeo begin both with a letter? [84]

ROMEO.

Ay, Nurse, what of that? Both with an R.

NURSE.

Ah, mocker! That's the dog's name; [85] R is for the —

---

78. **secret.** trustworthy
79. **keep counsel.** keep a secret
80. **prating.** babbling
81. **fain.** gladly. **lay knife aboard.** assert his claim.
 lief. willingly
82. **properer.** handsomer
83. **clout.** rag, cloth. **versal.** universal
84. **a letter.** one and the same letter
85. **the dog's name.** The letter _R_ was thought to resemble
 the dog's growl.

No; I know it begins with some other letter; and she hath the prettiest sententious [86] of it, of you and rosemary, that it would do you good to hear it.

ROMEO.
Commend me to thy lady.

NURSE.
Ay, a thousand times. [*Exit* ROMEO] Peter!

PETER.
Anon!

NURSE.
Before, and apace. [87]

[*Exit*]

---

86. sententious. The Nurse probably means sentences; clever, wise sayings.
87. Before, and apace. Go ahead quickly.

---◆---

Synopsis of Act II, Scene 4

In a square, Benvolio and Mercutio revealed that Tybalt had challenged Romeo to a duel. Mercutio made clever comments about Romeo's love for Rosaline and Tybalt's great concern about fencing etiquette. Romeo met his two friends, and he and Mercutio immediately began a duel of wits full of puns and clever wordplay. When the Nurse and her servant Peter joined them, Mercutio mocked her efforts to act like a lady. Then Mercutio and Benvolio went off, leaving Romeo with the Nurse. After giving the Nurse some money, Romeo explained that he had made plans with the Friar for a wedding the next day. He told the Nurse that he would send a rope ladder to her later so he could climb into Juliet's window on their wedding night.

---◆---

---◆---

Before You Read Act II, Scene 5

Like Romeo in Scene 3, Juliet is impatient to be married. Again, like Romeo, she is frustrated by the talk of an older person. However, notice the difference between the Nurse and the Friar. While Friar Laurence tried to advise Romeo, the Nurse is anything but serious. Although the Nurse enjoys teasing Juliet, she is sympathetic to the girl's feelings. Notice how she shows this. The Nurse is a dramatic contrast to Juliet, just as the Friar is a dramatic contrast to Romeo.

---◆---

ACT II. Scene 5.

Location: Verona. Outside Capulet's house,
perhaps in the orchard or garden.

[*Enter* JULIET]

JULIET.
  The clock struck nine when I did send the Nurse;
  In half an hour she promised to return.
  Perchance she cannot meet him. That's not so.
  O, she is lame! Love's heralds should be thoughts,
  Which ten times faster glide than the sun's beams
  Driving back shadows over louring hills. [1]
  Therefore do nimble-pinioned doves draw Love, [2]
  And therefore hath the wind-swift Cupid wings.
  Now is the sun upon the highmost hill
  Of this day's journey, and from nine till twelve
  Is three long hours, yet she is not come.
  Had she affections and warm youthful blood,   *Nurse has*
  She would be as swift in motion as a ball;   *no affection*
  My words would bandy her to my sweet love, [3]
  And his to me.
  But old folks, many feign as they were dead — [4]
  Unwieldy, slow, heavy, and pale as lead.

[*Enter* NURSE *and* PETER]

  O God, she comes! — O honey Nurse, what news?
  Hast thou met with him? Send thy man away.

---

1. **louring.** darkening, threatening
2. **Love.** Venus, whose chariot was drawn by swift-winged
   doves
3. **bandy.** toss back and forth
4. **feign as.** act as though

NURSE.
Peter, stay at the gate.

[*Exit* PETER]

JULIET.
Now, good sweet Nurse—O Lord, why lookest thou
    sad?
Though news be sad, yet tell them merrily;
If good, thou shamest the music of sweet news
By playing it to me with so sour a face.

NURSE.
I am aweary. Give me leave awhile. [5]
Fie, how my bones ache! What a jaunce have I had! [6]

JULIET.
I would thou hadst my bones, and I thy news.
Nay, come, I pray thee, speak. Good, good Nurse,
    speak.

NURSE.
Jesu, what haste! Can you not stay awhile? [7]
Do you not see that I am out of breath?

JULIET.
How art thou out of breath, when thou hast breath
To say to me that thou art out of breath?
The excuse that thou dost make in this delay
Is longer than the tale thou dost excuse.
Is thy news good or bad? Answer to that;

---

5. **Give me leave.** excuse me, let me alone a moment
6. **jaunce.** jolting trip
7. **stay.** wait

Say either, and I'll stay the circumstance. [8]
Let me be satisfied; Is 't good or bad?

NURSE.

Well, you have made a simple choice. You know
[9]not how to choose a man. Romeo? No, not he.
Though his face be better than any man's, yet his
leg excels all men's; and for a hand, and a foot, and a
body, though they be not to be talked on, [10] yet they
are past compare. He is not the flower of courtesy,
but, I'll warrant him, as gentle as a lamb. Go thy
ways, wench. Serve God. What, have you dined at
home?

JULIET.

No, no; but all this did I know before.
What says he of our marriage? What of that?

NURSE.

Lord, how my head aches! What a head have I!
It beats as it would fall in twenty pieces.
My back o' t'other side — ah, my back, my back! [11]
Beshrew your heart for sending me about [12]
To catch my death with jauncing up and down!

JULIET.

I' faith, I am sorry that thou art not well.
Sweet, sweet, sweet Nurse, tell me, what says my
    love?

---

  8. stay the circumstance. wait for the details
  9. simple. foolish
 10. be not to be talked on. are not worth discussing
 11. o' t'other. on the other
 12. Beshrew your heart. a mild oath

NURSE.
Your love says, like an honest gentleman,
And a courteous, and a kind, and a handsome,
And, I warrant, a virtuous —Where is your mother?

JULIET.
Where is my mother? Why, she is within,
Where should she be? How oddly thou repliest!
"Your love says, like an honest gentleman,
'Where is your mother?'"

NURSE.
                    O God's Lady dear!
Are you so hot? Marry, come up, I trow. [13]
Is this the poultice for my aching bones? [14]
Henceforward do your messages yourself.

JULIET.
Here's such a coil! Come, what says Romeo? [15]

NURSE.
Have you got leave to go to shrift today?

JULIET.
I have.

NURSE.
Then hie you hence to Friar Laurence' cell; [16]
There stays a husband to make you a wife.

---

13. **hot.** impatient.   **Marry, come up.** an expression of
    impatient reproof
14. **poultice.** remedy
15. **coil.** fuss, disturbance
16. **hie.** hurry

Now comes the wanton blood up in your cheeks; [17]
They'll be in scarlet straight at any news. [18]
Hie you to church. I must another way,
To fetch a ladder, by the which your love
Must climb a bird's nest soon when it is dark. [19]
I am the drudge, and toil in your delight,
But you shall bear the burden soon at night.
Go. I'll to dinner. Hie you to the cell.

JULIET.
Hie to high fortune! Honest Nurse, farewell.

[Exit separately]

---

17. wanton. excited
18. in scarlet straight. blushing immediately
19. bird's nest. Juliet's room

---◆---

Synopsis of Act II, Scene 5

For three hours, Juliet waited impatiently in the orchard for her Nurse to return from Romeo. When she did arrive, the Nurse teased Juliet by complaining about all her physical problems instead of giving the girl Romeo's message. Although irritated with the Nurse, Juliet kept her temper until the Nurse gave her Romeo's instructions: Juliet was to pretend to go to the Friar for confession. However, instead of confessing, the two were to be married.

---◆---

---◆---

Before You Read Act II, Scene 6

Notice the foreshadowing throughout this short scene. The Friar, sensing danger, warns that the lovers are too hasty. Note the lines that indicate that he has fears for the future. Romeo's words also foreshadow doom. Pay attention to the words of Romeo that remind us that disaster awaits.

Notice what Romeo says about Julieras she approaches. At the feast he described her as a shining light, and in the balcony scene he spoke of her as the sun. How does he describe her here?

---◆---

ACT II. Scene 6.

Location: Verona. Friar Laurence's cell.

[*Enter* FRIAR LAURENCE *and* ROMEO]

FRIAR LAURENCE.
So smile the heavens upon this holy act [1]
That after-hours with sorrow chide us not! [2]

ROMEO.
Amen, amen! But come what sorrow can,
It cannot countervail the exchange of joy [3]
That one short minute gives me in her sight.
Do thou but close our hands with holy words, [4]
Then love-devouring death do what he dare;
It is enough I may but call her mine.

FRIAR LAURENCE.
These violent delights have violent ends
And in their triumph die, like fire and powder, [5]
Which as they kiss consume. The sweetest honey
Is loathsome in his own deliciousness, [6]
And in the taste confounds the appetite. [7]
Therefore love moderately. Long love doth so;
Too swift arrives as tardy as too slow.

[*Enter* JULIET]

negative words

---

1. **So ... heavens.** may the heavens so smile
2. **chide.** punish
3. **countervail.** equal, counterbalance
4. **close.** join
5. **powder.** gunpowder
6. **his.** its
7. **confounds.** destroys

Here comes the lady. O, so light a foot
Will ne'er wear out the everlasting flint. [8]
A lover may bestride the gossamer [9]
That idles in the wanton summer air, [10]
And yet not fall; so light is vanity. [11]

JULIET.
Good even to my ghostly confessor. [12]

FRIAR LAURENCE.
Romeo shall thank thee, daughter, for us both. [13]

JULIET.
As much to him, else is his thanks too much. [14]

ROMEO.
Ah, Juliet, if the measure of thy joy
Be heaped like mine, and that thy skill be more [15]
To blazon it, then sweeten with thy breath [16]
This neighbor air, and let rich music's tongue
Unfold the imagined happiness that both [17]
Receive in either by this dear encounter. [18]

---

8. **flint.** stone
9. **gossamer.** spider's web
10. **wanton.** playful
11. **vanity.** transitory human love
12. **ghostly.** spiritual
13. **thank thee.** give a kiss in thanks for your greeting
14. **As ... much.** Then I greet him with a kiss in repayment.
15. **that.** if
16. **blazon.** describe, set forth
17. **Unfold.** make known. **imagined.** unexpressed
18. **in either.** from each other

JULIET.
Conceit, more rich in matter than in words, [19]
Brags of his substance, not of ornament.
They are but beggars that can count their worth.
But my true love is grown to such excess
I cannot sum up sum of half my wealth. [20]

FRIAR LAURENCE.
Come, come with me, and we will make short work;
For, by your leaves, you shall not stay alone
Till Holy Church incorporate two in one.

[Exit]

---

19. Conceit ... ornament. True understanding finds more
value in the substance of reality than in outward show.
20. sum up sum. add up the total

————————◆————————

Synopsis of Act II, Scene 6

While Romeo and the Friar waited for Juliet to arrive, the Friar warned Romeo that this love had been too hasty. Haste, he stressed, can cause disaster. Romeo agreed but announced that even death could not ruin his happiness. Juliet arrived, the lovers reaffirmed their love, and the Friar led them inside his cell for their marriage.

————————◆————————

---◆---

Before You Read Act III, Scene 1

The third act of a five act play is often the turning point, and Act III of *Romeo and Juliet* is no exception. Up until this scene, the story could have ended without tragedy if the marriage had been made public. However, the events of this scene make a happy ending impossible. Do you recall the fears of Juliet, Romeo, and the Friar? What they all feared is set in motion because of the hot-blooded natures of Tybalt and Mercutio. Notice that two of the characters, Benvolio and Romeo, try unsuccessfully to stop the coming disaster. Once the action has started, Romeo is dragged into action. He must avenge Mercutio.

Throughout this scene, be alert to Mercutio's wit and changeable personality. When he tells Benvolio "Thy head is as full of quarrels as an egg is full of meat," whom is he really describing? Notice also that his clever way with words does not desert him even in the end. He jokes and puns about his injuries. His only regret is that he received the blow from Tybalt, a man whom he hated. What curse does Mercutio make as he dies?

---◆---

ACT III. Scene 1.

Location: Verona. A public place.

[*Enter* MERCUTIO, BENVOLIO , *and men*]

BENVOLIO.
I pray thee, good Mercutio, let's retire.
The day is hot, the Capels are abroad, [1]
And if we meet we shall not scape a brawl,
For now, these hot days, is the mad blood stirring.

MERCUTIO.
Thou art like one of these fellows that when he
enters the confines of a tavern, claps me his sword
upon the table and says, "God send me no need of
thee!" and by the operation of the second cup draws
him on the drawer, [2] when indeed there is no need. [3]

BENVOLIO.
Am I like such a fellow?

MERCUTIO.
Come, come, thou art as hot a Jack [4] in thy mood as
any in Italy, and as soon moved to be moody, [5] and
as soon moody to be moved. [6]

BENVOLIO.
And what to?

---

1. **Capels.** Capulets
2. **draws ... drawer.** draws his sword against the
    bartender or waiter
3. **there is no need.** of his sword
4. **as hot a Jack.** as hot-tempered a person
5. **moody.** angry
6. **to be moved.** at being provoked

MERCUTIO.

Nay, an [7] there were two such, we should have none
shortly, for one would kill the other. Thou! Why,
thou wilt quarrel with a man that hath a hair more
or a hair less in his beard than thou hast. Thou wilt
quarrel with a man for cracking nuts, having no
other reason but because thou hast hazel eyes. What
eye but such an eye would spy out such a quarrel?
Thy head is as full of quarrels as an egg is full of
meat, [8] and yet thy head hath been beaten as addle [9]
as an egg for quarreling. Thou hast quarreled with a
man for coughing in the street, because he hath wak-
ened thy dog that hath lain asleep in the sun. Didst
thou not fall out with a tailor for wearing his new
doublet [10] before Easter? With another, for tying his
new shoes with old ribbon? And yet thou wilt tutor
me from quarreling! [11]

BENVOLIO.

An I were so apt to quarrel as thou art, any man
should buy the fee simple of my life for an hour and a
quarter. [12]

MERCUTIO.

The fee simple! O simple! [13]

[*Enter* TYBALT, PETRUCHIO, *and others*]

---

7. **an.** if
8. **meat.** edible matter
9. **addle.** addled, confused
10. **doublet.** man's jacket
11. **tutor ... quarreling.** tell me not to quarrel
12. **an hour ... quarter.** i.e., my life would last only an hour
    and fifteen minutes in such circumstances
13. **simple.** stupid

BENVOLIO.
By my head, here comes the Capulets.

MERCUTIO.
By my heel, I care not.

TYBALT.
[*To his companions*]
Follow me close, for I will speak to them. —
Gentlemen, good e'en. A word with one of you.

MERCUTIO.
And but one word with one of us? Couple it with
something: make it a word and a blow.

TYBALT.
You shall find me apt enough to that, sir, an you will
give me occasion. [14]

MERCUTIO.
Could you not take some occasion without giving?

TYBALT.
Mercutio, thou consortest [15] with Romeo.

MERCUTIO.
"Consort"? [16] what, dost thou make us minstrels? An
thou make minstrels of us, look to hear nothing but
discords. [17] Here's my fiddlestick; [18] here's that [19]
shall make you dance. Zounds, [20] "consort"!

---

14. **occasion.** cause, reason
15. **consortest.** keep company with
16. **Consort.** associate with; a group of musicians
17. **discords.** harsh sounds
18. **fiddlestick.** sword
19. **that.** that which
20. **Zounds.** by God's (Christ's) wounds

BENVOLIO.
We talk here in the public haunt of men.
Either withdraw unto some private place,
Or reason coldly of your grievances, [21]
Or else depart; here all eyes gaze on us. [22]

MERCUTIO.
Men's eyes were made to look, and let them gaze.
I will not budge for no man's pleasure, I.

[*Enter* ROMEO]

TYBALT.
Well, peace be with you, sir. Here comes my man. [23]

MERCUTIO.
But I'll be hanged, sir, if he wear your livery. [24]
Marry, go before to field, he'll be your follower; [25]
Your worship in that sense may call him "man." [26]

TYBALT.
Romeo, the love I bear thee can afford
No better term than this: thou art a villain. [27]

ROMEO.
Tybalt, the reason that I have to love thee
Doth much excuse the appertaining rage [28]

---

21. coldly. calmly
22. depart. go away separately
23. man. servant; here, the man Tybalt is looking for
24. livery. servant's uniform
25. field. place where a duel might occur
26. Your worship. a title of honor used here with mock
politeness
27. villain. low, vulgar person
28. appertaining. appropriate

To such a greeting. Villain am I none.
Therefore, farewell. I see thou knowest me not.

TYBALT.
Boy, this shall not excuse the injuries
That thou hast done me. Therefore turn and draw.

ROMEO.
I do protest I never injured thee,
But love thee better than thou canst devise [29]
Till thou shalt know the reason of my love.
And so, good Capulet—which name I tender [30]
As dearly as mine own—be satisfied.

MERCUTIO.
O calm, dishonorable, vile submission!
Alla stoccata carries it away. [31]

[*He draws*]

Tybalt, you ratcatcher, will you walk? [32]

TYBALT.
What wouldst thou have with me?

MERCUTIO.
Good king of cats, nothing but one of your nine lives,
that I mean to make bold withal, [33] and, as you shall
use me hereafter, dry-beat [34] the rest of the eight.
Will you pluck your sword out of his pilcher [35] by the

---

29. **devise.** understand
30. **tender.** value
31. ***Alla stoccata.*** at the thrust of the sword
32. **ratcatcher.** an allusion to Tybalt as king of cats
33. **make bold withal.** make free with, take
34. **dry-beat.** beat soundly without drawing blood
35. **his pilcher.** its scabbard

ears? Make haste, lest mine be about your ears ere
it be out.

TYBALT.
I am for you.

[He draws]

ROMEO.
Gentle Mercutio, put thy rapier up.

MERCUTIO.
Come, sir, your *passado*. [36]

[They fight]

ROMEO.
Draw, Benvolio, beat down their weapons.
Gentlemen, for shame, forbear this outrage!
Tybalt, Mercutio, the Prince expressly hath
Forbid this bandying in Verona streets.
Hold, Tybalt! Good Mercutio!

[TYBALT *under* ROMEO'S *arm*
stabs MERCUTIO.
Away TYBALT *with his followers*]

MERCUTIO.
I am hurt.
A plague o' both your houses! I am sped. [37]
Is he gone, and hath nothing?

BENVOLIO.
What, art thou hurt?

---

36. *passado*. forward thrust
37. sped. done for

MERCUTIO.
Ay, ay, a scratch, a scratch, marry, 'tis enough.
Where is my page? Go, villain, fetch a surgeon.

[*Exit* PAGE]

ROMEO.
Courage, man, the hurt cannot be much.

MERCUTIO.
No, 'tis not so deep as a well, nor so wide as a
church door, but 'tis enough, 'twill serve. Ask for
me
tomorrow, and you shall find me a grave man. I am
peppered, [38] I warrant, for this world. A plague o'
both your houses! Zounds, a dog, a rat, a mouse, a
cat, to scratch a man to death! A braggart, a rogue,
a villain, that fights by the book of arithmetic! [39]
Why the devil came you between us? I was hurt
under your arm.

not so bad
but I'll do
pun

ROMEO.
I thought all for the best.

MERCUTIO.
Help me into some house, Benvolio,
Or I shall faint. A plague o' both your houses!
They have made worm's meat of me. I have it, [40]
And soundly too. Your houses!

---

38. peppered. finished, done for
39. by ... arithmetic. by the numbers, as in a textbook on
   fencing
40. I have it. I have received my death blow.

[Exit, supported by BENVOLIO]

ROMEO.
This gentleman, the Prince's near ally, [41]
My very friend, hath got this mortal hurt [42]
In my behalf; my reputation stained
With Tybalt's slander — Tybalt, that an hour
Hath been my cousin! O sweet Juliet, [43]
Thy beauty hath made me effeminate, [44]
And in my temper softened valor's steel! [45]

Love weakened me

[Enter BENVOLIO]

BENVOLIO.
O Romeo, Romeo, brave Mercutio is dead!
That gallant spirit hath aspired the clouds, [46]
Which too untimely here did scorn the earth.

ROMEO.
This day's black fate on more days doth depend; [47]
This but begins the woe others must end. [48]

[Enter TYBALT]

BENVOLIO.
Here comes the furious Tybalt back again.

---

41. **ally.** kinsman
42. **very.** true
43. **cousin** kinsman
44. **effeminate.** weak
45. **temper.** disposition
46. **aspired.** ascended to
47. **depend.** hang over threateningly
48. **others.** other days to come

ROMEO.
Alive in triumph, and Mercutio slain!
Away to heaven, respective lenity, [49]
And fire-eyed fury be my conduct now! [50]
Now, Tybalt, take the "villain" back again
That late thou gavest me, for Mercutio's soul
Is but a little way above our heads,
Staying for thine to keep him company.
Either thou or I, or both, must go with him.

TYBALT.
Thou, wretched boy, that didst consort him here,
Shalt with him hence.

ROMEO.
                    This shall determine that.

                [They fight. TYBALT *falls]*

BENVOLIO.
Romeo, away, begone!
The citizens are up, and Tybalt slain.
Stand not amazed. The Prince will doom thee
    death [51]
If thou art taken. Hence, begone, away!

ROMEO.
O, I am fortune's fool! [52]

BENVOLIO.
                    Why dost thou stay?

---

49. respective lenity. thoughtful gentleness
50. conduct. guide
51. amazed. dazed.   **doom thee death.** sentence you to death
52. fool. dupe

[*Exit* ROMEO]

[*Enter* CITIZENS]

FIRST CITIZEN.
Which way ran he that killed Mercutio?
Tybalt, that murderer, which way ran he?

BENVOLIO.
There lies that Tybalt.

FIRST CITIZEN.
                    Up, sir, go with me.
I charge thee in the Prince's name, obey.

[*Enter* PRINCE *(attended), old* MONTAGUE,
CAPULET, *their* WIVES, *and all*]

PRINCE.
Where are the vile beginners of this fray?

BENVOLIO.
O noble Prince, I can discover all [53]
The unlucky manage of this fatal brawl. [54]
There lies the man, slain by young Romeo,
That slew thy kinsman, brave Mercutio.

CAPULET'S WIFE.
Tybalt, my cousin! O my brother's child!
O Prince! O cousin! Husband! O, the blood is
    spilled
Of my dear kinsman! Prince, as thou art true,
For blood of ours shed blood of Montague.
O cousin, cousin!

---

53. discover. reveal
54. manage. conduct

PRINCE.

Benvolio, who began this bloody fray?

BENVOLIO.

Tybalt, here slain, whom Romeo's hand did slay.
Romeo, that spoke him fair, bid him bethink [55]
How nice the quarrel was, and urged withal [56]
Your high displeasure. All this — utterèd
With gentle breath, calm look, knees humbly
    bowed —
Could not take truce with the unruly spleen [57]
Of Tybalt deaf to peace, but that he tilts
With piercing steel at bold Mercutio's breast,
Who, all as hot, turns deadly point to point,
And, with a martial scorn, with one hand beats
Cold death aside and with the other sends
It back to Tybalt, whose dexterity
Retorts it. Romeo he cries aloud, [58]
"Hold, friends! Friends, part!" and swifter than
    his tongue
His agile arm beats down their fatal points,
And twixt them rushes; underneath whose arm
An envious thrust from Tybalt hit the life [59]
Of stout Mercutio, and then Tybalt fled; [60]
But by and by comes back to Romeo,
Who had but newly entertained revenge, [61]

---

55. fair. civilly. **bethink.** consider
56. nice. trivial. **withal.** besides
57. take truce. make peace. **spleen.** angry nature
58. Retorts. returns
59. envious. full of hate
60. stout. brave
61. entertained. considered

And to 't they go like lightning, for, ere I
Could draw to part them was stout Tybalt slain,
And, as he fell, did Romeo turn and fly.
This is the truth, or let Benvolio die.

CAPULET'S WIFE.
He is a kinsman to the Montague.
Affection makes him false; He speaks not true. [62]
Some twenty of them fought in this black strife,
And all those twenty could but kill one life.
I beg for justice, which thou, Prince, must give.
Romeo slew Tybalt; Romeo must not live.

PRINCE.
Romeo slew him, he slew Mercutio.
Who now the price of his dear blood doth owe?

MONTAGUE.
Not Romeo, Prince, he was Mercutio's friend;
His fault concludes but what the law should end, [63]
The life of Tybalt.

PRINCE.
                              And for that offense
Immediately we do exile him hence.
I have an interest in your heart's proceeding;
My blood for your rude brawls doth lie a-bleeding; [64]
But I'll amerce you with so strong a fine [65]
That you shall all repent the loss of mine.

---

62. Affection. partiality
63. concludes but. only finishes
64. My blood. blood of my kinsman
65. amerce. punish

I will be deaf to pleading and excuses;
Nor tears nor prayers shall purchase out abuses. [66]
Therefore use none. Let Romeo hence in haste, [67]
Else, when he is found, that hour is his last. [68]
Bear hence this body and attend our will. [69]
Mercy but murders, pardoning those that kill.

[*Exit, some carrying* TYBALT'*s body*]

---

66. Nor tears. neither tears   **purchase out abuses.**
   make up for misdeeds
67. hence. depart
68. Else. otherwise
69. attend our will. wait for my judgment

Synopsis of Act III, Scene 1

On the same day as the wedding, Benvolio and Mercutio were walking through Verona when they were challenged by a group of Capulets led by Tybalt. Tybalt, who was searching for Romeo, accused Mercutio of being friendly with the young Montague. Mercutio, who was as excitable and hot-tempered as Tybalt, replied sharply. A quarrel broke out in spite of Benvolio's efforts to calm things down. As the quarrel heated to a boiling point, Romeo arrived. Tybalt directed his insults at Romeo, but Romeo tried to avoid a fight. Mercutio thought Romeo was being cowardly. He provoked Tybalt into continuing the original quarrel. The two dueled. Mercutio fell, receiving a mortal injury under the arm of Romeo who was trying to stop the fight. Romeo could no longer hold his temper. He felt he had to avenge his friend's death. He and Tybalt fought and Tybalt was killed. Soon the Prince was notified. As a punishment, Romeo was banished.

Before You Read Act III, Scene 2

Compare the beginning of this scene to Act II, Scene 5. Here, Shakespeare uses dramatic irony. Juliet is again impatient and eager. Now we feel pity for her because she does not know what has happened to Romeo.

The Nurse adds to the suspense of the scene for she is upset and cannot explain to Juliet clearly what has happened. What is Juliet's first reaction when she finally understands the Nurse? What does she say next?

ACT III. Scene 2.

Location: Verona. Capulet's house.

[*Enter* JULIET *alone*] *light*

JULIET.
  Gallop apace, you fiery-footed steeds, [1]
  Towards Phoebus' lodging! Such a wagoner [2]
  As Phaethon would whip you to the west
  And bring in cloudy night immediately.
  Spread thy close curtain, love-performing night, [3]
  That runaways' eyes may wink, and Romeo [4]
  Leap to these arms, untalked of and unseen.
  Lovers can see to do their amorous rites
  By their own beauties; or, if love be blind,
  It best agrees with night. Come, civil night, [5]
  Thou sober-suited matron all in black.

  *

  Hood my unmanned blood, bating in my cheeks, [6]

---

1. **apace.** quickly.   **steeds.** the horses of the sun god's chariot
2. **Phoebus.** the sun god.   **lodging.** in the west, below the horizon. **such ... Phaethon** a rash charioteer like Phaethon, who would quickly bring the day to an end. Phaethon was son of the sun god, and was allowed to assume the reins of the sun for a day; not being able to restrain the steeds, he had to be slain by the thunderbolt of Zeus.
3. **close.** enclosing
4. **runaways' ... wink.** so that the eyes of busybodies cannot see
5. **civil.** courteous, dignified
6. **Hood.** cover, a term in falconry; the hawk's eyes were covered so that it would not bate or beat its wings. **unmanned.** untamed

With thy black mantle till strange love grow bold, [7]
Think true love acted simple modesty. [8]
Come, night. Come, Romeo. Come, thou day in night;
For thou wilt lie upon the wings of night
Whiter than new snow upon a raven's back.
Come, gentle night, come, loving, black-browed night,
Give me my Romeo, and when I shall die
Take him and cut him out in little stars,
And he will make the face of heaven so fine
That all the world will be in love with night
And pay no worship to the garish sun. [9]
O, I have bought the mansion of a love [10]
But not possessed it, and though I am sold,
Not yet enjoyed. So tedious is this day
As is the night before some festival
To an impatient child that hath new robes
And may not wear them. O, here comes my nurse,

[*Enter* NURSE, *with cords*] [11]

And she brings news, and every tongue that speaks
But Romeo's name speaks heavenly eloquence.
Now, Nurse, what news? What hast thou there? The
cords
That Romeo bid thee fetch?

NURSE.

Ay, ay, the cords.

[*She throws them down*]

---

7. **strange.** unfamiliar
8. **Think.** and think
9. **garish.** dazzling
10. **mansion.** dwelling
11. **cords.** ropes for the ladder

JULIET.
Ay me, what news? Why dost thou wring thy
hands?

NURSE.
Ah, weraday! He's dead, he's dead, he's dead! [12]
We are undone, lady, we are undone!
Alack the day, he's gone, he's killed, he's dead!

JULIET.
Can heaven be so envious? [13]

NURSE.
                    Romeo can,
Though heaven cannot. O Romeo, Romeo!
Whoever would have thought it? Romeo!

JULIET.
What devil art thou, that dost torment me thus?
This torture should be roared in dismal hell.
Hath Romeo slain himself? Say thou but "Ay," [14]
And that bare vowel "I" shall poison more [15]
Than the death-darting eye of cockatrice. [16]
I am not I, if there be such an "Ay,"

---

12. **weraday.** wellaway, alas
13. **envious.** malicious
14. **Ay.** yes
15. **"I".** pronounced identically with "ay"
16. **cockatrice.** basilisk, a mythical serpent that could kill
    by its look
17. **those eyes shut.** if Romeo's eyes are shut in death

Or those eyes shut, that makes thee answer "Ay." [17]
If he be slain, say "Ay," or if not, "No."
Brief sounds determine of my weal or woe. [18]

NURSE.
I saw the wound. I saw it with mine eyes —
God save the mark! — here on his manly breast. [19]
A piteous corpse, a bloody piteous corpse;
Pale, pale as ashes, all bedaubed in blood,
All in gore-blood. I swoonèd at the sight. [20]

JULIET.
O, break, my heart! Poor bankrupt, break at once!
To prison, eyes; ne'er look on liberty!
Vile earth, to earth resign; end motion here, [21]
And thou and Romeo press one heavy bier! [22]

NURSE.
O Tybalt, Tybalt, the best friend I had!
O courteous Tybalt! Honest gentleman!
That ever I should live to see thee dead!

JULIET.
What storm is this that blows so contrary? [23]
Is Romeo slaughtered, and is Tybalt dead?
My dearest cousin, and my dearer lord?
Then, dreadful trumpet, sound the general doom! [24]
For who is living, if those two are gone?

---

18. **weal.** welfare, happiness
19. **God save the mark.** God save us from evil.
20. **gore-blood.** clotted blood
21. **Vile ... resign.** let my body return to the earth
22. **press.** weigh down.   **bier.** litter for carrying corpses
23. **contrary.** in opposite directions
24. **trumpet** the last trumpet.   **general doom.** Day of Judgment

NURSE.

Tybalt is gone, and Romeo banishèd;
Romeo that killed him, he is banishèd.

JULIET.

O God! Did Romeo's hand shed Tybalt's blood?

NURSE.

It did, it did. Alas the day it did!

JULIET.

O serpent heart, hid with a flowering face! [25]
Did ever dragon keep so fair a cave? [26]
Beautiful tyrant! Fiend angelical!
Dove-feathered raven! wolvish-ravening lamb!
Despisèd substance of divinest show! [27]
Just opposite to what thou justly seem'st, [28]
A damnèd saint, an honorable villain!
O nature, what hadst thou to do in hell
When thou didst bower the spirit of a fiend [29]
In mortal paradise of such sweet flesh?
Was ever book containing such vile matter
So fairly bound? O, that deceit should dwell
In such a gorgeous palace!

(handwritten margin note: oxymorons – like Romeo talking about love)

NURSE.

There's no trust,
No faith, no honesty in men; all perjured,

---

25. hid with. hidden by. **flowering.** fair, like that of the
serpent in the Garden of Eden
26. keep. occupy, guard. **cave.** one with treasure in it
27. show. appearance
28. Just. precisely (with a play on justly, truly)
29. bower. give lodging to

All forsworn, all naught, all dissemblers. [30]
Ah, where's my man? Give me some aqua vitae. [31]
These griefs, these woes, these sorrows make me old.
Shame come to Romeo!

JULIET.
> Blistered be thy tongue
For such a wish! He was not born to shame.
Upon his brow shame is ashamed to sit;
For 'tis a throne where honor may be crowned
Sole monarch of the universal earth.
O, what a beast was I to chide at him!

NURSE.
Will you speak well of him that killed your cousin?

JULIET.
Shall I speak ill of him that is my husband?
Ah, poor my lord, what tongue shall smooth thy name [32]
When I, thy three-hours wife, have mangled it?
But wherefore, villain, didst thou kill my cousin?
That villain cousin would have killed my husband.
Back, foolish tears, back to your native spring!
Your tributary drops belong to woe, [33]
Which you, mistaking, offer up to joy.
My husband lives, that Tybalt would have slain, [34]
And Tybalt's dead, that would have slain my husband.

---

30. naught. worthless, evil. **dissemblers.** hypocrites,
phonies
31. aqua vitae. alcoholic spirits
32. poor my lord. Romeo. **smooth.** speak kindly of
33. Your ... woe. Your tears should be shed, offered as a
tribute, on some occasion of real grief.
34. that. whom

All this is comfort. Wherefore weep I then?
Some word there was, worser than Tybalt's death,
That murdered me. I would forget it fain, [35]
But O, it presses to my memory
Like damnèd guilty deeds to sinners' minds:
"Tybalt is dead, and Romeo-banishèd."
That "banishèd," that one word "banishèd,"
Hath slain ten thousand Tybalts. Tybalt's death
Was woe enough, if it had ended there;
Or, if sour woe delights in fellowship
And needly will be ranked with other griefs, [36]
Why followed not, when she said "Tybalt's dead,"
"Thy father," or "thy mother," nay, or both,
Which modern lamentation might have moved? [37]
But with a rearward following Tybalt's death, [38]
"Romeo is banishèd" — to speak that word
Is father, mother, Tybalt, Romeo, Juliet,
All slain, all dead. "Romeo is banishèd!"
There is no end, no limit, measure, bound,
In that word's death; no words can that woe sound. [39]
Where is my father and my mother, Nurse?

NURSE.
Weeping and wailing over Tybalt's corpse.
Will you go to them? I will bring you thither.

---

35. fain. gladly
36. needly. of necessity. **ranked with.** accompanied by
37. modern. ordinary. **lamentation.** funeral cry
38. rearward. rearguard
39. sound. express

JULIET.

Wash they his wounds with tears? Mine shall be spent,
When theirs are dry, for Romeo's banishment.
Take up those cords. Poor ropes, you are beguiled,
Both you and I, for Romeo is exiled.
He made you for a highway to my bed;
But I, a maid, die maiden-widowèd.
Come, cords, come, Nurse. I'll to my wedding bed,
And death, not Romeo, take my maidenhead!

NURSE.

   [*Taking up the cords*]
Hie to your chamber. I'll find Romeo
To comfort you. I wot well where he is. ⁴⁰
Hark ye, your Romeo will be here at night.
I'll to him. He is hid at Laurence' cell.

JULIET.

O, find him! Give this ring to my true knight,

[*Giving a ring*]

And bid him come to take his last farewell.

[*Exit separately*]

---

40. wot. know

———————◆———————

Synopsis of Act III, Scene 2

In the Capulet orchard, Juliet waited impatiently for the Nurse. The Nurse was extremely upset when she arrived. Along with Romeo's rope ladder, she brought terrible news. The Nurse was so frantic that, at first, it seemed to Juliet that Romeo had been murdered. Juliet's grief was somewhat lessened when she learned that it was Tybalt who had been killed. When she discovered that Romeo had killed her beloved cousin, Juliet reacted childishly and condemned her new husband. Then, she quickly took back her words and expressed her loyalty to Romeo in a mature manner. However, Romeo's banishment was a terrible blow to her. The Nurse did give her some good news. Romeo, the Nurse revealed, was hiding in the Friar's cell. Juliet immediately sent the old woman to ask that Romeo come to her room that evening.

———————◆———————

———————◆———————

Before You Read Act III, Scene 3

Here Romeo receives the news of his fate from the Friar. As you read this scene, compare the reactions of Romeo to those of Juliet and the behavior of the Friar to that of the Nurse. Notice how the youthful Romeo reacts much more emotionally to the news of his banishment than the Friar who sees the punishment as a "gentler judgment." Consider what this scene shows about the character of Romeo. Even the Nurse, who is long-winded and babbling, becomes impatient with Romeo's behavior. Notice how Shakespeare creates dramatic irony in this scene with one word as Romeo refers to his love for Juliet. What word is it?

———————◆———————

ACT III. Scene 3.

Location: Verona. Friar Laurence's cell.

[*Enter* FRIAR LAURENCE]

FRIAR LAURENCE.
Romeo, come forth; come forth, thou fearful man. [1]
Affliction is enamored of thy parts, [2]
And thou art wedded to calamity.

[*Enter* ROMEO]

ROMEO.
Father, what news? What is the Prince's doom? [3]
What sorrow craves acquaintance at my hand
That I yet know not?

FRIAR LAURENCE.
                    Too familiar
Is my dear son with such sour company.
I bring thee tidings of the Prince's doom.

ROMEO.
What less than doomsday is the Prince's doom? [4]

FRIAR LAURENCE.
A gentler judgment vanished from his lips: [5]
Not body's death, but body's banishment.

---

1. **fearful.** full of fear
2. **parts.** qualities
3. **doom.** judgment
4. **doomsday.** the Day of Judgment, death
5. **vanished.** issued into air

ROMEO.
Ha, banishment? Be merciful, say "death";
For exile hath more terror in his look,
Much more than death. Do not say "banishment."

FRIAR LAURENCE.
Here from Verona art thou banished.
Be patient, for the world is broad and wide.

ROMEO.
There is no world without Verona walls [6]
But purgatory, torture, hell itself.
Hence "banishèd" is banished from the world,
And world's exile is death. Then "banishèd" [7]
Is death mistermed. Calling death "banishèd,"
Thou cutt'st my head off with a golden ax
And smilest upon the stroke that murders me.

FRIAR LAURENCE.
O deadly sin! O rude unthankfulness!
Thy fault our law calls death, but the kind Prince, [8]
Taking thy part, hath rushed aside the law [9]
And turned that black word "death" to
    "banishment."
This is dear mercy, and thou seest it not.

ROMEO.
'Tis torture, and not mercy. Heaven is here
Where Juliet lives, and every cat and dog

---

6. **without.** outside of
7. **world's exile.** exile from the world
8. **Thy fault ... death.** For your crime our law demands
   the death penalty.
9. **rushed.** pushed aside

And little mouse, every unworthy thing,
Live here in heaven and may look on her,
But Romeo may not. More validity, [10]
More honorable state, more courtship lives [11]
In carrion flies than Romeo. They may seize
On the white wonder of dear Juliet's hand
And steal immortal blessing from her lips,
Who even in pure and vestal modesty [12]
Still blush, as thinking their own kisses sin; [13]
But Romeo may not, he is banishèd.
Flies may do this, but I from this must fly.
They are free men, but I am banishèd.
And sayest thou yet that exile is not death?
Hadst thou no poison mixed, no sharp-ground knife,
No sudden mean of death, though ne'er so mean, [14]
But "banishèd" to kill me? "Banishèd"?
O Friar, the damned use that word in hell;
Howling attends it. How hast thou the heart,
Being a divine, a ghostly confessor,
A sin absolver, and my friend professed,
To mangle me with that word "banishèd"?

FRIAR LAURENCE.
Thou fond mad man, hear me a little speak. [15]

ROMEO.
O, thou wilt speak again of banishment.

---

10. **validity.** value
11. **courtship.** courtliness; occasion for wooing
12. **vestal.** maidenly
13. **their own kisses.** their touching one another
14. **mean ... mean.** method, means ... humiliating, base
15. **fond.** foolish

FRIAR LAURENCE.
I'll give thee armor to keep off that word,
Adversity's sweet milk, philosophy,
To comfort thee, though thou art banishèd.

ROMEO.
Yet "banishèd"? Hang up philosophy! [16]
Unless philosophy can make a Juliet,
Displant a town, reverse a prince's doom, [17]
It helps not, it prevails not. Talk no more.

FRIAR LAURENCE.
O, then I see that madmen have no ears.

ROMEO.
How should they, when that wise men have no eyes?

FRIAR LAURENCE.
Let me dispute with thee of thy estate. [18]

ROMEO.
Thou canst not speak of that thou dost not feel. [19]
Wert thou as young as I, Juliet thy love,
An hour but married, Tybalt murderèd,
Doting like me and like me banishèd,
Then mightst thou speak, then mightst thou tear thy
    hair,
And fall upon the ground, as I do now,
Taking the measure of an unmade grave.
                    [*He falls upon the ground*]

---

16. **Yet.** still
17. **Displant.** uproot
18. **dispute.** reason. **estate.** situation
19. **that.** that which

[Knock within]

FRIAR LAURENCE.
Arise. One knocks. Good Romeo, hide thyself.

ROMEO.
Not I, unless the breath of heartsick groans,
Mistlike, infold me from the search of eyes.

[Knock]

FRIAR LAURENCE.
Hark, how they knock! — Who's there? — Romeo,
  arise.
Thou wilt be taken. — Stay awhile! — Stand up.

[Knock]

Run to my study. — By and by! — God's will, [20]
What simpleness is this? — I come, I come! [21]

[Knock]

Who knocks so hard? Whence come you? What's
  your will?

[Going to the door]

NURSE.
  [Within]
Let me come in, and you shall know my errand.
I come from Lady Juliet.

FRIAR LAURENCE.
                    Welcome, then.
                    [He opens the door]

---

20. By and by. in a minute
21. simpleness. foolishness

[*Enter* NURSE]

NURSE.
O holy Friar, O, tell me, holy Friar,
Where's my lady's lord, where's Romeo?

FRIAR LAURENCE.
There on the ground, with his own tears made
   drunk.

NURSE.
O, he is even in my mistress' case, [22]
Just in her case! O woeful sympathy! [23]
Piteous predicament! Even so lies she,
Blubbering and weeping, weeping and
   blubbering.—
Stand up, stand up! Stand, an you be a man. [24]
For Juliet's sake, for her sake, rise and stand!
Why should you fall into so deep an O? [25]

ROMEO.
Nurse!
                                       [*He rises*]

NURSE.
Ah, sir, ah, sir! Death's the end of all.

ROMEO.
Spakest thou of Juliet? How is it with her?

---

22. even. exactly. **case.** situation
23. woeful sympathy. shared grief
24. an. if
25. an O. a fit of grief

Doth not she think me an old murderer, [26]
Now I have stained the childhood of our joy
With blood removed but little from her own?
Where is she? And how doth she? And what says
My concealed lady to our canceled love? [27]

NURSE.
O, she says nothing, sir, but weeps and weeps,
And now falls on her bed, and then starts up,
And "Tybalt" calls, and then on Romeo cries, [28]
And then down falls again.

ROMEO.
                    As if that name,
Shot from the deadly level of a gun, [29]
Did murder her, as that name's cursèd hand
Murdered her kinsman. O, tell me, Friar, tell me,
In what vile part of this anatomy
Doth my name lodge? Tell me, that I may sack [30]
The hateful mansion.

[He draws a weapon, but is restrained]

FRIAR LAURENCE.
                    Hold thy desperate hand!
Art thou a man? Thy form cries out thou art;
Thy tears are womanish, thy wild acts denote
The unreasonable fury of a beast.

---

26. **old.** hardened
27. **concealed.** secret.   **canceled.** stopped by the
    impending exile
28. **on Romeo cries.** exclaims against Romeo, calls his name
29. **level.** aim
30. **sack.** destroy, plunder

Unseemly woman in a seeming man, [31]
And ill-beseeming beast in seeming both!
Thou hast amazed me. By my holy order,
I thought thy disposition better tempered. [32]
Hast thou slain Tybalt? Wilt thou slay thyself,
And slay thy lady, that in thy life lives,
By doing damnèd hate upon thyself?
Why railest thou on thy birth, the heaven, and earth,
Since birth, and heaven, and earth, all three do meet [33]
In thee at once, which thou at once wouldst lose?
Fie, fie, thou shamest thy shape, thy love, thy wit, [34]
Which, like a usurer, abound'st in all, [35]
And usest none in that true use indeed [36]
Which should bedeck thy shape, thy love, thy wit. [37]
Thy noble shape is but a form of wax, [38]
Digressing from the valor of a man; [39]
Thy dear love sworn but hollow perjury,
Killing that love which thou hast vowed to cherish; [40]
Thy wit, that ornament to shape and love,
Misshapen in the conduct of them both, [41]

---

31. **Unseemly.** inappropriate, unnatural
32. **tempered.** balanced, even
33. **heaven, and earth.** soul and body
34. **wit.** intellect
35. **Which ... all.** who, like a rich money lender, possesses
    all capabilities
36. **true use.** proper use of your resources, not usury
37. **bedeck.** do honor to
38. **form of wax.** waxwork, outer form
39. **Digressing.** if it deviates
40. **Killing.** if it kills
41. **conduct.** guidance

Like powder in a skilless soldier's flask [42]
Is set afire by thine own ignorance,
And thou dismembered with thine own defense. [43]
What, rouse thee, man! Thy Juliet is alive,
For whose dear sake thou wast but lately dead; [44]
There art thou happy. Tybalt would kill thee, [45]
But thou slewest Tybalt; there art thou happy.
The law that threatened death becomes thy friend
And turns it to exile; there art thou happy.
A pack of blessings light upon thy back,
Happiness courts thee in her best array,
But like a mishavèd and sullen wench [46]
Thou pouts upon thy fortune and thy love.
Take heed, take heed, for such die miserable.
Go, get thee to thy love, as was decreed;
Ascend her chamber; hence and comfort her.
But look thou stay not till the watch be set, [47]
For then thou canst not pass to Mantua,
Where thou shalt live till we can find a time
To blaze your marriage, reconcile your friends, [48]
Beg pardon of the Prince, and call thee back
With twenty hundred thousand times more joy
Than thou went'st forth in lamentation.
Go before, Nurse. Commend me to thy lady,
And bid her hasten all the house to bed,

---

42. **powder.** gunpowder. **flask.** powder horn
43. **dismembered ... defense.** Your wit or intellect is
    destroying rather than helping you.
44. **wast ... dead.** only recently were wishing yourself dead
45. **happy.** fortunate
46. **mishavèd.** misbehaved. **wench.** low, common girl
47. **the watch be set.** guards be posted at the gates
48. **blaze.** announce publicly. **friends.** relations

Which heavy sorrow makes them apt unto. [49]
Romeo is coming.

NURSE.
O Lord, I could have stayed here all the night
To hear good counsel. O, what learning is! —
My lord, I'll tell my lady you will come.

ROMEO.
Do so, and bid my sweet prepare to chide.

NURSE.
   [*Giving a ring*]
Here, sir, a ring she bid me give you, sir.
Hie you, make haste, for it grows very late.

                     [*Exit*]

ROMEO.
How well my comfort is revived by this! [50]

FRIAR LAURENCE.
Go hence. Good night. And here stands all your
   state: [51]
Either be gone before the watch be set,
Or by the break of day disguised from hence.
Sojourn in Mantua. I'll find out your man, [52]
And he shall signify from time to time [53]

---

49. apt unto. likely to do
50. comfort. happiness
51. here ... state. your future depends on what follows
52. Sojourn. stay
53. signify. let you know

Every good hap to you that chances here. [54]
Give me thy hand. 'Tis late. Farewell, good night.

ROMEO.
But that a joy past joy calls out on me,
It were a grief so brief to part with thee. [55]
Farewell.

[Exit separately]

---

54. good hap. fortunate event
55. brief. quickly

---◆---

Synopsis of Act III, Scene 3

At the Friar's cell, Romeo frantically complained about his situation. Friar Laurence tried to console him, but Romeo would not be consoled. He threw himself on the floor in a great show of despair. At this point, the Nurse entered, bringing news of Juliet. The Friar called Romeo's behavior woman-like and scolded Romeo, pointing out that the situation could be much worse. Indeed, the Friar had a plan. Romeo would meet Juliet as planned and then leave the city for Mantua before dawn. There he would stay until it was safe to return to Verona.

---◆---

———————◆———————

Before You Read Act III, Scene 4

This scene is another reminder that fate interferes in the lives of these "star-cross'd lovers." Capulet makes arrangements for Paris to marry Juliet while she is spending her wedding night with Romeo on the floor above. (It was the custom for parents to arrange marriages during this period.) However, Capulet's sudden decision to marry Juliet to Paris without her consent seems surprising since previously he said that Juliet must agree: "My will to her consent is but a part." Why does Capulet change his mind? Is it fate at work?

———————◆———————

ACT III. Scene 4.

Location: Verona. Capulet's house.

[*Enter old* CAPULET, *his* WIFE, *and* PARIS]

CAPULET.
Things have fallen out, sir, so unluckily [1]
That we have had no time to move our daughter. [2]
Look you, she loved her kinsman Tybalt dearly,
And so did I. Well, we were born to die.
'Tis very late. She'll not come down tonight.
I promise you, but for your company [3]
I would have been abed an hour ago.

PARIS.
These times of woe afford no times to woo.
Madam, good night. Commend me to your daughter.

WIFE.
I will, and know her mind early tomorrow.
Tonight she's mewed up to her heaviness. [4]

dramatic irony

CAPULET.
Sir Paris, I will make a desperate tender [5]
Of my child's love. I think she will be ruled
In all respects by me; nay, more, I doubt it not.
Wife, go you to her ere you go to bed.
Acquaint her here of my son Paris' love, [6]

---

1. **fallen out.** happened
2. **move.** persuade, discuss the proposal with
3. **promise.** assure
4. **mewed up to.** cooped up with.   **heaviness.** sorrow
5. **desperate tender.** risky offer
6. **son.** son-in-law

And bid her, mark you me, on Wednesday next — [7]
But soft, what day is this?

PARIS.

Monday, my lord.

CAPULET.

Monday! Ha, ha! well, Wednesday is too soon;
O' Thursday let it be. O' Thursday, tell her, [8]
She shall be married to this noble earl.
Will you be ready? Do you like this haste?
We'll keep no great ado — a friend or two; [9]
For hark you, Tybalt being slain so late, [10]
It may be thought we held him carelessly, [11]
Being our kinsman, if we revel much.
Therefore we'll have some half a dozen friends,
And there an end. But what say you to Thursday?

PARIS.
My lord, I would that Thursday were tomorrow.

CAPULET.
Well, get you gone. O' Thursday be it, then.
[*To his* WIFE] Go you to Juliet ere you go to bed;
Prepare her, wife, against this wedding day. — [12]
Farewell, my lord. — Light to my chamber, ho! —

---

7. **mark you me.** are you paying attention
8. **O'.** on
9. **ado.** fuss
10. **late.** recently
11. **held him carelessly.** did not respect him highly
12. **against.** in anticipation of

Afore me, it is so very late [13]
That we may call it early by and by.
Good night.

[Exit]

---

13. Afore me. by my life, a mild oath

---◆---

Synopsis of Act III, Scene 4

On Monday, the Capulets discussed with Paris the idea of his proposed marriage to Juliet. At first the Capulets rejected the idea because it was so soon after Tybalt's death. Just as Paris was leaving, Capulet changed his mind. A marriage would get Juliet's mind off her cousin's death, he thought. Juliet, her parents believed, would follow their wishes, and the couple would be married Thursday. A delighted Paris departed.

---◆---

Before You Read Act III, Scene 5

The scene begins quietly with the lovers delaying their separation by talking. Notice how Juliet alternates between being a child and a woman. At first, she selfishly wants to keep Romeo with her. The next moment she rushes him out because she fears for his life. Be alert to Romeo's continued use of the light and dark imagery that he has used throughout the play. Note what Juliet sees as Romeo leaves. Notice the Capulets' reaction to Juliet's refusal to marry Paris. Ask yourself what their actions say about them. Juliet's conversation with her mother is full of double meanings. We understand her meanings but Lady Capulet does not. Shakespeare again has used dramatic irony.

The role of the Nurse changes a great deal in this scene. Earlier, the Nurse was Juliet's confidante. What happens to the relationship here? Notice that the Nurse, being older, realizes that a person should not defy authority. Juliet, of course, disagrees. The Nurse is only trying to bring peace to the family, but Juliet interprets it differently. What other character has been trying to create harmony?

ACT III. Scene 5.

Location: Verona. Capulet's orchard with Juliet's chamber window above, and s ubsequently the interior of Juliet's chamber.

[*Enter* ROMEO *and* JULIET *aloft at the window*]

JULIET.
Wilt thou be gone? It is not yet near day.
It was the nightingale, and not the lark, [1]
That pierced the fearful hollow of thine ear; [2]
Nightly she sings on yond pomegranate tree.
Believe me, love, it was the nightingale.

ROMEO.
It was the lark, the herald of the morn,
No nightingale. Look, love, what envious streaks
Do lace the severing clouds in yonder east. [3]
Night's candles are burnt out, and jocund day [4]
Stands tiptoe on the misty mountain tops.
I must be gone and live, or stay and die.

JULIET.
Yond light is not daylight, I know it, I.
It is some meteor that the sun exhaled [5]
To be to thee this night a torchbearer

---

1. **nightingale ... lark.** nightingales were associated with night, larks with dawn
2. **fearful.** apprehensive, anxious
3. **severing.** separating, parting
4. **jocund.** cheerful
5. **exhaled.** sent out

And light thee on thy way to Mantua.
Therefore stay yet. Thou need'st not to be gone.

ROMEO.

Let me be ta'en; let me be put to death.
I am content, so thou wilt have it so. ⁶
I'll say yon gray is not the morning's eye;
'Tis but the pale reflex of Cynthia's brow. ⁷
Nor that is not the lark whose notes do beat
The vaulty heaven so high above our heads.
I have more care to stay than will to go. ⁸
Come, death, and welcome! Juliet wills it so.
How is 't, my soul? Let's talk. It is not day.

JULIET.

It is, it is. Hie hence, begone, away! ⁹
It is the lark that sings so out of tune,
Straining harsh discords and unpleasing sharps. ¹⁰
Some say the lark makes sweet division; ¹¹
This doth not so, for she divideth us.
Some say the lark and loathèd toad changed eyes; ¹²
O, now I would they had changed voices too,
Since arm from arm that voice doth us affray, ¹³

---

6. **so thou.** if you
7. **reflex.** reflection. **Cynthia's.** the moon's
8. **care.** desire, concern
9. **Hie hence.** hurry away
10. **sharps.** notes high in pitch and shrill
11. **division.** variations on a melody
12. **changed.** exchanged; a popular saying, to account for the
   observation that the lark has very ordinary eyes and a
   beautiful body, while the toad has remarkable eyes but an
   ugly body
13. **arm from arm.** from one another's arms. **affray.** frighten

Hunting thee hence with hunt's-up to the day. [14]
O, now begone! More light and light it grows.

ROMEO.
More light and light, more dark and dark our woes!

[*Enter* NURSE *hastily*]

NURSE.
Madam!

JULIET.
Nurse?

NURSE.
Your lady mother is coming to your chamber.
The day is broke; be wary, look about.

[*Exit*]

JULIET.
Then window, let day in, and let life out.

ROMEO.
Farewell, farewell! One kiss, and I'll descend.

[*They kiss. He climbs down from the window*]

JULIET.
Art thou gone so? Love, lord, ay, husband, friend! [15]
I must hear from thee every day in the hour,
For in a minute there are many days.

---

14. hunt's-up. a song or tune to awaken huntsmen or a
newly married couple
15. friend. lover

O, by this count I shall be much in years [16]
Ere I again behold my Romeo!

ROMEO.
[*From below her window*] Farewell!
I will omit no opportunity
That may convey my greetings, love, to thee.

JULIET.
O, think'st thou we shall ever meet again?

ROMEO.
I doubt it not, and all these woes shall serve
For sweet discourses in our times to come. [17]

JULIET.
O God, I have an ill-divining soul! [18]
Methinks I see thee, now thou art so low,
As one dead in the bottom of a tomb.
Either my eyesight fails or thou lookest pale.

ROMEO.
And trust me, love, in my eye so do you.
Dry sorrow drinks our blood. Adieu, adieu! [19]

[*Exit*]

JULIET.
O Fortune, Fortune! All men call thee fickle.
If thou art fickle, what dost thou with him [20]

---

16. **count.** method of calculation.   **much in years.** very old
17. **discourses.** conversations
18. **ill-divining.** predicting evil
19. **Dry ... blood.** The heat of the body in sorrow and despair
    was thought to dry up the blood.
20. **dost thou.** do you have to do

That is renowned for faith? Be fickle, Fortune.
For then, I hope, thou wilt not keep him long,
But send him back.

[*Enter* MOTHER (CAPULET'S WIFE)]

WIFE.

                    Ho, daughter, are you up?

JULIET.

Who is 't that calls? It is my lady mother.
Is she not down so late, or up so early? [21]
What unaccustomed cause procures her hither? [22]

                    [*She goeth down from the window*]

WIFE.

Why, how now, Juliet?

JULIET.

                    Madam, I am not well.

WIFE. - *thinks & looks stupid*

Evermore weeping for your cousin's death?
What, wilt thou wash him from his grave with tears?
An if thou couldst, thou couldst not make him live; [23]
Therefore, have done. Some grief shows much of
     love,
But much of grief shows still some want of wit. [24]

---

21. **down.** in bed
22. **procures ... hither.** brings her here
23. **An if.** if
24. **wit.** intellect

JULIET.
Yet let me weep for such a feeling loss. [25]

WIFE.
So shall you feel the loss, but not the friend
Which you weep for.

JULIET.
Feeling so the loss,
I cannot choose but ever weep the friend.

WIFE.
Well, girl, thou weep'st not so much for his death
As that the villain lives which slaughtered him.

JULIET.
What villain, madam?

WIFE.
That same villain, Romeo.

JULIET.
[*Aside*]
Villain and he be many miles asunder. — [26]
God pardon him! I do, with all my heart;
And yet no man like he doth grieve my heart. [27]

WIFE.
That is because the traitor murderer lives.

---

25. **feeling.** deeply felt
26. **asunder.** apart
27. **no man like he.** no man so much as he.
  grieve. anger, grieve with longing. Juliet speaks to her
  mother throughout in intentional ambiguities.

JULIET.

Ay, madam, from the reach of these my hands.
Would none but I might venge my cousin's death!

WIFE.

We will have vengeance for it, fear thou not.
Then weep no more. I'll send to one in Mantua,
Where that same banished runagate doth live, [28]
Shall give him such an unaccustomed dram [29]
That he shall soon keep Tybalt company.
And then, I hope, thou wilt be satisfied.

JULIET.

Indeed, I never shall be satisfied
With Romeo till I behold him — dead —
Is my poor heart so for a kinsman vexed.
Madam, if you could find out but a man
To bear a poison, I would temper it, [30]
That Romeo should, upon receipt thereof,
Soon sleep in quiet. O, how my heart abhors
To hear him named, and cannot come to him
To wreak the love I bore my cousin [31]
Upon his body that hath slaughtered him! [32]

WIFE.

Find thou the means, and I'll find such a man.
But now I'll tell thee joyful tidings, girl.

---

28. runagate. renegade, fugitive
29. Shall. who shall.   **dram.** dose; one-eighth of a fluid
   ounce
30. temper. mix, concoct; alloy, dilute
31. wreak. avenge; express
32. his body that. the body of him who

JULIET.

And joy comes well in such a needy time.
What are they, beseech your ladyship?

WIFE.

Well, well, thou hast a careful father, child, [33]
One who, to put thee from thy heaviness, [34]
Hath sorted out a sudden day of joy [35]
That thou expects not, nor I looked not for.

JULIET.

Madam, in happy time! What day is that? [36]

WIFE.

Marry, my child, early next Thursday morn, [37]
The gallant, young, and noble gentleman,
The County Paris, at Saint Peter's Church
Shall happily make thee there a joyful bride.

JULIET.

Now, by Saint Peter's Church, and Peter too,
He shall not make me there a joyful bride!
I wonder at this haste, that I must wed
Ere he that should be husband comes to woo.
I pray you, tell my lord and father, madam,
I will not marry yet, and when I do I swear
It shall be Romeo, whom you know I hate,
Rather than Paris. These are news indeed!

---

33. **careful.** considerate
34. **heaviness.** sorrow
35. **sorted out.** chosen
36. **in happy time.** just in time
37. **Marry.** by the Virgin Mary

WIFE.

Here comes your father. Tell him so yourself,
And see how he will take it at your hands.

[*Enter* CAPULET *and* NURSE]

CAPULET.

When the sun sets, the earth doth drizzle dew,
But for the sunset of my brother's son
It rains downright.
How now, a conduit, girl? What, still in tears? [38]
Evermore showering? In one little body
Thou counterfeits a bark, a sea, a wind; [39]
For still thy eyes, which I may call the sea,
Do ebb and flow with tears; the bark thy body is,
Sailing in this salt flood; the winds, thy sighs,
Who, raging with thy tears, and they with them,
Without a sudden calm, will overset [40]
Thy tempest-tossèd body. — How now, wife?
Have you delivered to her our decree?

WIFE.

Ay, sir, but she will none, she gives you thanks. [41]
I would the fool were married to her grave!

CAPULET.

Soft, take me with you, take me with you, wife. [42]
How? Will she none? Doth she not give us thanks?

---

38. conduit. water pipe, fountain
39. bark. sailing vessel
40. Without ... calm. unless they quickly calm themselves
41. will ... thanks. says "no thank you," she'll have no part
of it
42. take ... you. let me understand you

Is she not proud? Doth she not count her blest, [43]
Unworthy as she is, that we have wrought [44]
So worthy a gentleman to be her bride? [45]

JULIET.
Not proud you have, but thankful that you have.
Proud can I never be of what I hate,
But thankful even for hate that is meant love. [46]

good intentions

CAPULET.
How, how, how, how, chopped logic? What is this? [47]
"Proud," and "I thank you," and "I thank you not,"
And yet "not proud"? Mistress minion, you, [48]
Thank me no thankings, nor proud me no prouds,
But fettle your fine joints 'gainst Thursday next [49]
To go with Paris to Saint Peter's Church,
Or I will drag thee on a hurdle thither. [50]
Out, you greensickness carrion! Out, you baggage! [51]
You tallow-face!

Joan girl? why so mean

WIFE.
[*To* CAPULET] Fie, fie! What, are you mad? [52]

---

43. **proud.** pleased.   **count her.** consider herself
44. **wrought.** procured
45. **bride.** bridegroom
46. **hate ... love.** that which is horrible but which was meant lovingly
47. **chopped logic.** contradictory, shallow argument
48. **minion.** spoiled darling, minx
49. **fettle.** prepare.   **'gainst.** in anticipation of
50. **a hurdle.** a sled on which criminals were dragged to execution
51. **greensickness.** an anemic ailment of young unmarried women.   **baggage.** good-for-nothing
52. **tallow-face.** pale-face

JULIET.
[*Kneeling*]
Good father, I beseech you on my knees,
Hear me with patience but to speak a word.

CAPULET. *authority is questioned*
Hang thee, young baggage, disobedient wretch!
I tell thee what: get thee to church o' Thursday
Or never after look me in the face.
Speak not, reply not, do not answer me!
My fingers itch. Wife, we scarce thought us blest
That God had lent us but this only child;
But now I see this one is one too much,
And that we have a curse in having her.
Out on her, hilding!

NURSE.
God in heaven bless her! [53]
You are to blame, my lord, to rate her so. [54]

CAPULET.
And why, my Lady wisdom? Hold your tongue,
Good Prudence. Smatter with your gossips, go. [55]

NURSE.
I speak no treason.

CAPULET.
O, God-i'-good-e'en! [56]

---

53. hilding. worthless person
54. rate. berate, scold
55. Smatter. chatter
56. God-i'-good-e'en. for God's sake

NURSE.
May not one speak?

CAPULET.
                    Peace, you mumbling fool!
Utter your gravity o'er a gossip's bowl, [57]
For here we need it not.

WIFE.
You are too hot. *your face gets hot when you're angry*

CAPULET.
God's bread, it makes me mad! [58]
Day, night, hour, tide, time, work, play, [59]
Alone, in company, still my care hath been
To have her matched. And having now provided
A gentleman of noble parentage,
Of fair demesnes, youthful, and nobly liened, [60]
Stuffed, as they say, with honorable parts, [61]
Proportioned as one's thought would wish a man —
And then to have a wretched puling fool, [62]
A whining mammet, in her fortune's tender, [63]
To answer, "I'll not wed, I cannot love,
I am too young; I pray you, pardon me."
But, an you will not wed, I'll pardon you. [64]

---

57. **gravity.** wisdom
58. **God's bread.** by God's (Christ's) Sacrament
59. **tide.** season
60. **demesnes.** estates. **liened.** descended
61. **parts.** qualities
62. **puling.** whining
63. **mammet.** doll. **in ... tender.** when an offer of good
      fortune is made to her
64. **pardon you.** allow you to depart

Graze where you will, you shall not house with me.
Look to 't, think on 't. I do not use to jest. [65]
Thursday is near. Lay hand on heart; advise. [66]
An you be mine, I'll give you to my friend;
An you be not, hang, beg, starve, die in the streets,
For, by my soul, I'll ne'er acknowledge thee,
Nor what is mine shall never do thee good.
Trust to 't, bethink you. I'll not be forsworn. [67]

[Exit]

JULIET.
Is there no pity sitting in the clouds.
That sees into the bottom of my grief?
O sweet my Mother, cast me not away!
Delay this marriage for a month, a week;
Or if you do not, make the bridal bed
In that dim monument where Tybalt lies. *suicide*

WIFE.
Talk not to me, for I'll not speak a word.
Do as thou wilt, for I have done with thee.

[Exit]

JULIET.
O God! —O Nurse, how shall this be prevented?
My husband is on earth, my faith in heaven. [68]
How shall that faith return again to earth,

---

65. do not use. am not accustomed
66. advise. consider carefully
67. be forsworn. go back on my word
68. my faith in heaven. Juliet refers to her marriage vows
that are recorded in heaven.

Unless that husband send it me from heaven
By leaving earth? Comfort me, counsel me. [69]
Alack, alack, that heaven should practice
    stratagems [70]
Upon so soft a subject as myself!
What sayst thou? Hast thou not a word of joy?
Some comfort, Nurse.

NURSE. ~~changedsides~~

                Faith, here it is.
Romeo is banished, and all the world to nothing [71]
That he dares ne'er come back to challenge you, [72]
Or if he do, it needs must be by stealth.
Then, since the case so stands as now it doth,
I think it best you married with the County.
O, he's a lovely gentleman!
Romeo's a dishclout to him. An eagle, madam, [73]
Hath not so green, so quick, so fair an eye [74]
As Paris hath. Beshrew my very heart, [75]
I think you are happy in this second match,
For it excels your first; or if it did not,
Your first is dead—or 'twere as good he were,
As living here and you no use of him. [76]

JULIET.
Speak'st thou from thy heart?

---

69. leaving earth. dying
70. practice. scheme, contrive. **stratagems.** tricks, plots
71. all ... nothing. the odds are overwhelming
72. challenge. claim
73. dishclout. dishrag
74. quick. alert
75. Beshrew. cursed be
76. here. on earth

NURSE.
And from my soul too. Else beshrew them both.

JULIET.
Amen! [77]

NURSE.
What?

JULIET.
Well, thou hast comforted me marvelous much.
Go in, and tell my lady I am gone,
Having displeased my father, to Laurence' cell
To make confession and to be absolved. [78]

NURSE.
Marry, I will; and this is wisely done.

[*Exit*]

JULIET.
Ancient damnation! O most wicked fiend! [79]
Is it more sin to wish me thus forsworn, [80]
Or to dispraise my lord with that same tongue
Which she hath praised him with above compare
So many thousand times? Go, counselor,
Thou and my bosom henceforth shall be twain. [81]
I'll to the Friar to know his remedy.
If all else fail, myself have power to die.

[*Exit*]

soliloquy

---

77. Amen. Yes, indeed, beshrew (cursed be) your heart and soul.
78. be absolved. receive forgiveness for sins
79. Ancient damnation. damnable old woman
80. forsworn. be false to my marriage vows
81. bosom. private thoughts.   **twain.** separated

Synopsis of Act III, Scene 5

Romeo and Juliet were in her room the morning after their wedding. Juliet argued that it was still night, so Romeo did not have to leave yet. (Remember that Romeo had been banished and must leave Verona before daybreak.) At first, Romeo insisted that it was time for him to go, and then he agreed to stay. Suddenly realizing the danger he was in, Juliet changed her mind and urged him to leave before he could be found and executed.

The Nurse entered and warned that Lady Capulet was coming to see Juliet. Romeo climbed down the rope ladder, and the lovers said their last good-bye. Juliet feared for their future, saying "O, think'st thou we shall ever meet again?"

When her mother arrived, Juliet blamed her appearance on grief over Tybalt's death. Thinking that Juliet wanted to avenge her cousin's death, Lady Capulet suggested poisoning Romeo. Then, hoping to cheer Juliet up, Lady Capulet told her about the plans for her marriage to Paris on Thursday.

Capulet joined his wife and daughter. When Juliet refused to agree to the wedding, her father lost his temper and bawled her out. He even threatened to throw her out of the house. Lady Capulet offered no comfort to the girl. In fact, she wished that Juliet "were married to her grave." We know that this wish will soon come true. Lady Capulet left Juliet's room. Next Juliet turned to the Nurse, who suggested that Paris was a better man and she should marry him after all. Isolated from her parents and the Nurse, Juliet looked for the Friar for help.

Before You Read Act IV, Scene 1

Scene 1 is about halfway through the time span of the play. Juliet met Romeo on Sunday, married him on Monday, and in two days she will be dead.

Again Shakespeare has created parallel scenes. Compare Romeo's meeting with the Friar to that of Juliet. Both came to him because they received no help or understanding from their families. They trust his judgment, and both hope he will offer a solution to their predicaments.

Notice Juliet's self-control here. Observe the character of Paris in this scene. He is genuinely concerned about her pain and obviously cares for her.

There is a dramatic change in mood after Paris leaves. Notice the statements of Juliet create a picture of death. Be aware that many of Juliet's lines predict what is going to happen to her and to Romeo. Notice also how the Friar's skill with herbs, first mentioned in Act II, Scene 3, now becomes important. Remember what he said about good sometimes becoming evil. How does this happen in Romeo and Juliet?

ACT IV. Scene 1.

Location: Verona. Friar Laurence's cell.

[*Enter* FRIAR LAURENCE *and* COUNTY PARIS]

FRIAR LAURENCE.
On Thursday, sir? The time is very short.

PARIS.
My father Capulet will have it so, [1]
And I am nothing slow to slack his haste. [2]

FRIAR LAURENCE.
You say you do not know the lady's mind?
Uneven is the course. I like it not. [3]

PARIS.
Immoderately she weeps for Tybalt's death,
And therefore have I little talked of love,
For Venus smiles not in a house of tears. [4]
Now, sir, her father counts it dangerous
That she do give her sorrow so much sway,
And in his wisdom hastes our marriage [5]
To stop the inundation of her tears, [6]

---

1. **father.** future father-in-law
2. **nothing ... haste.** not at all reluctant in a way that might slacken his haste
3. **Uneven ... course.** The plan is irregular.
4. **Venus ... tears.** (1) Amorousness isn't appropriate in a house of mourning. (2) The planet Venus does not exert a favorable influence when it is in an inauspicious house or portion of the zodiac.
5. **hastes.** hurries
6. **inundation.** flood

Which, too much minded by herself alone, [7]
May be put from her by society. [8]
Now do you know the reason of this haste.

FRIAR LAURENCE.
    [*Aside*]
I would I knew not why it should be slowed. —*aside*
Look, sir, here comes the lady toward my cell.

[*Enter* JULIET]

PARIS.
Happily met, my lady and my wife!

JULIET.
That may be, sir, when I may be a wife.

PARIS.
That "may be" must be, love, on Thursday next.

JULIET.
What must be shall be.

FRIAR LAURENCE.
                    That's a certain text. [9]

PARIS.
Come you to make confession to this father?

JULIET.
To answer that, I should confess to you.

---

7. **minded.** thought about
8. **society.** companionship
9. **text.** truth

PARIS.

Do not deny to him that you love me.

JULIET.

I will confess to you that I love him.

PARIS.

So will ye, I am sure, that you love me.

JULIET.

If I do so, it will be of more price, [10] *does she mean that*

Being spoke behind your back, than to your face.

PARIS.

Poor soul, thy face is much abused with tears.

JULIET.

The tears have got small victory by that,

For it was bad enough before their spite. [11]

PARIS.

Thou wrong'st it more than tears with that report.

JULIET.

That is no slander, sir, which is a truth;

And what I spake, I spake it to my face. [12]

PARIS.

Thy face is mine, and thou hast slandered it.

JULIET.

It may be so, for it is not mine own. — *it's Romeo's*

---

10. **more price.** greater worth
11. **spite.** malice
12. **to my face.** (1) openly (2) about my face

Are you at leisure, holy Father, now,
Or shall I come to you at evening Mass?

FRIAR LAURENCE.

My leisure serves me, pensive daughter, now. [13]
My lord, we must entreat the time alone. [14]

PARIS.

God shield I should disturb devotion! [15]
Juliet, on Thursday early will I rouse ye.
Till then, adieu, and keep this holy kiss.

[*Exit*]

JULIET.

O, shut the door! And when thou hast done so,
Come weep with me—past hope, past cure, past
    help!

FRIAR LAURENCE.

Ah, Juliet, I already know thy grief;
It strains me past the compass of my wits. [16]
I hear thou must, and nothing may prorogue it, [17]
On Thursday next be married to this county.

JULIET.

Tell me not, Friar, that thou hearest of this,
Unless thou tell me how I may prevent it.
If in thy wisdom thou canst give no help,
Do thou but call my resolution wise

---

13. **pensive.** sorrowful
14. **entreat ... alone.** ask you to leave us alone
15. **shield.** prevent (that)
16. **strains.** forces. **compass.** bounds
17. **may prorogue.** can delay

And with this knife I'll help it presently. [18]

      suicide   [*She shows a knife*]

God joined my heart and Romeo's, thou our hands;
And ere this hand, by thee to Romeo's sealed,
Shall be the label to another deed, [19]
Or my true heart with treacherous revolt
Turn to another, this shall slay them both. [20]
Therefore, out of thy long-experienced time, [21]
Give me some present counsel, or, behold,
Twixt my extremes and me this bloody knife [22]
Shall play the umpire, arbitrating that [23]
Which the commission of thy years and art [24]
Could to no issue of true honor bring.
Be not so long to speak; I long to die [25]
If what thou speak'st speak not of remedy.

FRIAR LAURENCE.

Hold, daughter. I do spy a kind of hope,
Which craves as desperate an execution [26]
As that is desperate which we would prevent.
If, rather than to marry County Paris,
Thou hast the strength of will to slay thyself,
Then is it likely thou wilt undertake

---

18. **presently.** at once
19. **label.** strip attached to a deed to carry the seal; hence, confirmation, seal
20. **both.** hand and heart
21. **time.** age
22. **extremes.** extreme misfortunes
23. **arbitrating.** deciding
24. **commission.** authority. **art.** skill
25. **so long.** so slow
26. **craves.** requires

A thing like death to chide away this shame,
That cop'st with Death himself to scape from it; [27]
And if thou darest, I'll give thee remedy.

JULIET.
O, bid me leap, rather than marry Paris,
From off the battlements of any tower,
Or walk in thievish ways, or bid me lurk [28]
Where serpents are; chain me with roaring bears,
Or hide me nightly in a charnel house, [29]
O'ercovered quite with dead men's rattling bones,
With reeky shanks and yellow chopless skulls; [30]
Or bid me go into a new-made grave
And hide me with a dead man in his tomb —
Things that, to hear them told, have made me
    tremble —
And I will do it without fear or doubt,
To live an unstained wife to my sweet love.

FRIAR LAURENCE.
Hold, then. Go home, be merry, give consent
To marry Paris. Wednesday is tomorrow.
Tomorrow night look that thou lie alone;
Let not the Nurse lie with thee in thy chamber.
Take thou this vial, being then in bed,
                    [*Showing her a vial*]
And this distilling liquor drink thou off, [31]

---

27. **That cop'st.** you who would encounter or negotiate; or, a
    thing that would cope.   **it.** i.e., shame
28. **thievish ways.** roads frequented by thieves
29. **charnel house.** vault for human bones
30. **reeky.** reeking, malodorous.   **chopless.** without the
    lower jaw
31. **distilling.** infusing

When presently through all thy veins shall run
A cold and drowsy humor; for no pulse [32]
Shall keep his native progress, but surcease; [33]
No warmth, no breath shall testify thou livest;
The roses in thy lips and cheeks shall fade
To wanny ashes, thy eyes' windows fall [34]
Like death when he shuts up the day of life;
Each part, deprived of supple government, [35]
Shall, stiff and stark and cold, appear like death.
And in this borrowed likeness of shrunk death
Thou shalt continue two-and-forty hours,
And then awake as from a pleasant sleep.
Now, when the bridegroom in the morning comes
To rouse thee from thy bed, there art thou dead.
Then, as the manner of our country is,
In thy best robes uncovered on the bier [36]
Thou shalt be borne to that same ancient vault
Where all the kindred of the Capulets lie.
In the meantime, against thou shalt awake, [37]
Shall Romeo by my letters know our drift, [38]
And hither shall he come; and he and I
Will watch thy waking, and that very night
Shall Romeo bear thee hence to Mantua.
And this shall free thee from this present shame,

---

32. **humor.** fluid, moisture
33. **his native.** its natural.   **surcease.** cease
34. **wanny.** wan, pale.   **eye's windows.** eyelids
35. **supple government.** control of motion
36. **uncovered ... bier.** displayed on a funeral platform
37. **against.** before
38. **drift.** plan

Fr. Larry has a concoction that allows Juliet to "die" for 42 hrs - long enough to skip a wedding, while being prepared for her funeral, she'll wake up and run off with Romeo.

If no inconstant toy nor womanish fear [39]
Abate thy valor in the acting it. [40]

JULIET.
[*Taking the vial*]
Give me, give me! O, tell not me of fear!

FRIAR LAURENCE. *lets someone else handle it*
Hold, get you gone. Be strong and prosperous [41]
In this resolve. I'll send a friar with speed
To Mantua, with my letters to thy lord.

JULIET.
Love give me strength, and strength shall help
    afford. [42]
Farewell, dear Father!

[*Exit separately*]

---

39. toy. idle whim
40. Abate thy valor. lessen your courage
41. prosperous. successful
42. help afford. provide help

---◆---

Synopsis of Act IV, Scene 1

Paris visited the Friar's cell to plan for the wedding on Thursday. Because the Friar knew the true situation, he offered reasons to delay the marriage. However, Paris explained that Capulet insisted on the date to ease Juliet's grieving.

Juliet then entered and showed great self-control as she talked cleverly with Paris. After the Friar asked Paris to leave them alone, the mood abruptly changed. Juliet told the Friar that the only solution she saw was death. Because the Friar was an expert on herbs and medicines, he suggested another solution. Juliet was to take a potion the night before her wedding to Paris. It would make her appear dead. Meanwhile, the Friar would tell Romeo about the plan, and he would be there when Juliet awoke. Juliet agreed immediately and left with the potion.

---◆---

---◆---

Before You Read Act IV, Scene 2

Notice the dramatic irony in this scene. The Capulets are preparing for a wedding, and we know that Juliet is preparing for death. There is also irony in Juliet's words: "I met the youthful lord at Laurence's cell;/ And gave him what becomèd love I might./ Not stepping o'er the bounds of modesty." What is Juliet really saying? Notice Juliet's mood. What has happened to change it? How do her parents misinterpret her mood?

---◆---

ACT IV. Scene 2.

Location: Verona. Capulet's house.

[*Enter* FATHER CAPULET, MOTHER
(CAPULET'S WIFE), NURSE, *and*
SERVINGMEN, *two or three*]

CAPULET.
So many guests invite as here are writ.

[*Exit one or two* SERVINGMEN]

Sirrah, go hire me twenty cunning cooks. [1]

SERVINGMAN.
You shall have none ill, [2] sir, for I'll try [3] if they can
lick their fingers.

CAPULET.
How canst thou try them so?

SERVINGMAN.
Marry, sir, 'tis an ill cook that cannot lick his own
fingers; [4] therefore he that cannot lick his fingers
goes not with me.

CAPULET.
Go, begone.

[*Exit* SERVINGMAN]

---

1. **cunning.** skillful
2. **none ill.** no bad ones
3. **try.** test, check
4. **'tis ... fingers.** It's a bad cook who won't lick his own
   fingers.

We shall be much unfurnished for this time. [5]
What, is my daughter gone to Friar Laurence?

NURSE.
Ay, forsooth. [6]

CAPULET.
Well, he may chance to do some good on her.
A peevish self-willed harlotry it is. [7]

[*Enter* JULIET]

NURSE.
See where she comes from shrift with merry look.

CAPULET.
How now, my headstrong, where have you been
    gadding? [8]

JULIET.
Where I have learned me to repent the sin
Of disobedient opposition
To you and your behests, and am enjoined [9]
By holy Laurence to fall prostrate here, [10]
                    [*Kneeling*]
To beg your pardon. Pardon, I beseech you!
Henceforward I am ever ruled by you.

---

5. **unfurnished.** unprovided, unprepared
6. **forsooth.** in truth
7. **A peevish ... is.** It is ill-tempered, selfish behavior of a
   lower-class woman.
8. **gadding.** wandering
9. **behests.** commands. **enjoined.** commanded, instructed
10. **fall prostrate.** lie face down in submission

CAPULET.
Send for the County! Go tell him of this.
I'll have this knot knit up tomorrow morning.

JULIET.
I met the youthful lord at Laurence' cell
And gave him what becomèd love I might, [11]
Not stepping o'er the bounds of modesty.

I showed him the right amount of love-not too much though

CAPULET.
Why, I am glad on 't. This is well. Stand up.

[*JULIET rises*]

This is as 't should be. Let me see the County;
Ay, marry, go, I say, and fetch him hither.
Now, afore God, this reverend holy friar,
All our whole city is much bound to him. [12]

JULIET.
Nurse, will you go with me into my closet [13]
To help me sort such needful ornaments [14]
As you think fit to furnish me tomorrow?

WIFE.
No, not till Thursday. There is time enough.

CAPULET.
Go, Nurse, go with her. We'll to church tomorrow.

The wedding tomorrow

[*Exit JULIET and NURSE*]

---

11. **becomèd.** befitting, proper
12. **bound.** indebted
13. **closet.** private room
14. **sort.** choose. **ornaments.** clothes

WIFE.

We shall be short in our provision. [15]
'Tis now near night.

CAPULET.

Tush, I will stir about,
And all things shall be well, I warrant thee, wife.
Go thou to Juliet, help to deck up her. [16]
I'll not to bed tonight. Let me alone.
I'll play the huswife for this once. — What ho! — [17]
They are all forth. Well, I will walk myself
To County Paris, to prepare up him
Against tomorrow. My heart is wondrous light,
Since this same wayward girl is so reclaimed.

[*Exit*]

---

15. **short ... provision.** without time to prepare
16. **deck up.** dress, get ready
17. **huswife.** housewife.   **What ho!** a call to the servants

---◆---

Synopsis of Act IV, Scene 2

The Capulets, the Nurse, and the servants were preparing for the wedding ceremonies. Juliet returned from the Friar's cell. She seemed sorry for her disobedience, and asked her father to forgive her. Capulet was so pleased that he moved the wedding day up to Wednesday. Lady Capulet objected that this hasty date did not allow time to prepare. Capulet, however, stated that he would stay up all night to get ready and to tell Paris the news.

---◆---

———————◆———————

Before You Read Act IV, Scene 3

Juliet asks to be alone. She says that she must say her prayers since she is in a sinful state. We understand her meaning, but the Nurse cannot. Juliet then delivers a long and poetic speech. This speech shows us that Juliet accepts responsibility for what she is about to do. What else does this speech reveal that Juliet is thinking?

———————◆———————

ACT IV. Scene 3.

Location: Verona. Capulet's house; Juliet's bed, enclosed by bedcurtains, is thrust out or is otherwise visible.

[*Enter* JULIET *and* NURSE]

JULIET.
Ay, those attires are best. But, gentle Nurse,
I pray thee, leave me to myself tonight;
For I have need of many orisons [1]
To move the heavens to smile upon my state, [2]
Which, well thou knowest, is cross and full of sin. [3]

[*Enter* MOTHER (CAPULET'S WIFE)].

WIFE.
What, are you busy, ho? Need you my help?

JULIET.
No, madam, we have culled such necessaries [4]
As are behooveful for our state tomorrow. [5]
So please you, let me now be left alone,
And let the Nurse this night sit up with you,
For I am sure you have your hands full all
In this so sudden business.

WIFE.
                    Good night.
Get thee to bed and rest, for thou hast need.

---

1. **orisons.** prayers
2. **state.** condition
3. **cross.** disobedient, selfish
4. **culled.** picked, chosen
5. **behooveful.** appropriate, correct.   **state.** ceremony

[*Exit* CAPULET'S WIFE *and* NURSE].

JULIET.
Farewell! God knows when we shall meet again.
I have a faint cold fear thrills through my veins [6]
That almost freezes up the heat of life.
I'll call them back again to comfort me.
Nurse! —What should she do here?
My dismal scene I needs must act alone.
Come, vial.
                              [*She takes out the vial*]
What if this mixture do not work at all?
Shall I be married then tomorrow morning?
No, no, this shall forbid it. Lie thou there.
                              [*She lays down a dagger*]
What if it be a poison which the Friar
Subtly hath ministered to have me dead, [7]
Lest in this marriage he should be dishonored
Because he married me before to Romeo?
I fear it is; and yet methinks it should not,
For he hath still been tried a holy man. [8]
How if, when I am laid into the tomb,
I wake before the time that Romeo
Come to redeem me? There's a fearful point!
Shall I not then be stifled in the vault,
To whose foul mouth no healthsome air breathes in,
And there die strangled ere my Romeo comes?
Or, if I live, is it not very like, [9]
The horrible conceit of death and night, [10]
Together with the terror of the place —

6. **faint.** producing faintness.   **thrills.** pierces, shivers
7. **ministered.** given me
8. **still.** always.   **tried.** proved
9. **like.** likely
10. **conceit.** idea

As in a vault, an ancient receptacle, [11]
Where for this many hundred years the bones
Of all my buried ancestors are packed;
Where bloody Tybalt, yet but green in earth, [12]
Lies festering in his shroud; where, as they say,
At some hours in the night spirits resort —
Alack, alack, is it not like that I, [13]
So early waking, what with loathsome smells,
And shrieks like mandrakes torn out of the earth, [14]
That living mortals, hearing them, run mad — [15]
O, if I wake, shall I not be distraught, [16]
Environèd with all these hideous fears, [17]
And madly play with my forefathers' joints,
And pluck the mangled Tybalt from his shroud,
And in this rage, with some great kinsman's bone [18]
As with a club dash out my desperate brains?
O, look! Methinks I see my cousin's ghost *Shakespearean*
Seeking out Romeo, that did spit his body [19]
Upon a rapier's point. Stay, Tybalt, stay! [20]
Romeo, Romeo, Romeo! Here's drink — I drink to thee.

foreshadowing death

[*She drinks and falls upon her bed,
within the curtains*]

---

11. **As.** namely
12. **green.** new, freshly
13. **like.** likely
14. **mandrakes.** The forked root of the mandrake resembled
    the human form; the plant was thought to utter a shriek
    when torn from the ground.
15. **That.** so that
16. **distraught.** mentally ill
17. **Environèd.** surrounded.   **fears.** objects of fear
18. **rage.** madness.   **great.** of an earlier generation, an
    ancestor
19. **spit.** spear
20. **Stay.** stop

---◆---

Synopsis of Act IV, Scene 3

Tuesday, the night before the wedding, Juliet and the Nurse chose the outfit she would wear the next day. Juliet then asked her mother and the Nurse to leave her alone that night so she could pray.

When she was alone, she expressed fears that the potion would not work correctly. If it did not work at all, Juliet would use a dagger to kill herself. Then she feared that the potion was poison, but she rejected that notion. Finally, she imagined all the horrors that she would face if she awoke alone in the tomb. While thinking these dreadful thoughts, she thought that she saw Tybalt's ghost searching for its slayer, Romeo. Finally, she drank the potion and fell onto her bed.

---◆---

———————◆———————

Before You Read Act IV, Scene 4

Contrast this scene with the previous one. Notice that this scene is full of life and bustling humor. We know that the potion, in the meantime, is making Juliet's blood settle and her body grow cold. Why do you think Shakespeare included this scene?

———————◆———————

ACT IV. Scene 4.

Location: Scene continues. Juliet's bed remains visible.

[*Enter* LADY OF THE HOUSE (CAPULET'S WIFE) *and* NURSE]

WIFE.
Hold, take these keys, and fetch more spices, Nurse.

NURSE.
They call for dates and quinces in the pastry. [1]

[*Enter old* CAPULET]

CAPULET.
Come, stir, stir, stir! The second cock hath crowed.
The curfew bell hath rung; 'tis three o'clock.
Look to the baked meats, good Angelica. [2]
Spare not for cost.

NURSE.
                    Go, you cotquean, go, [3]
Get you to bed. Faith, you'll be sick tomorrow
For this night's watching. [4]

CAPULET.
No, not a whit. What, I have watched ere now
All night for lesser cause, and ne'er been sick.

---

1. **quinces.** golden, apple-shaped fruit. **pastry.** room in
    which pastry was made
2. **baked meats.** pies, pastry. **Angelica.** probably the
    Nurse's name.
3. **cotquean.** a man who acts the housewife
4. **watching.** being awake, staying awake

WIFE.
Ay, you have been a mouse-hunt in your time, [5]
But I will watch you from such watching now. [6]

[*Exit* LADY *and* NURSE]

CAPULET.
A jealous hood, a jealous hood! [7]

[*Enter three or four* SERVINGMEN *with spits and logs, and baskets*]

Now, fellow, what is there?

FIRST SERVINGMAN.
Things for the cook, sir, but I know not what.

CAPULET.
Make haste, make haste. [*Exit* FIRST SERVING
MAN] Sirrah, fetch drier logs.
Call Peter. He will show thee where they are.

SECOND SERVINGMAN
I have a head, sir, that will find out logs
And never trouble Peter for the matter.

CAPULET.
Mass, and well said. [8]*
Thou shalt be loggerhead. [*Exit* SERVINGMAN]
Good faith, 'tis day. [9]

---

5. mouse-hunt. i.e., hunter of women
6. watch ... watching. i.e., keep an eye on you to prevent such nighttime activity
7. A jealous hood. i.e., you wear the cap of jealousy
8. Mass. by the Mass
9. loggerhead. a blockhead

The County will be here with music straight, [10]
For so he said he would. I hear him near.

[Play music within]

Nurse! Wife! what ho! What, Nurse, I say!

[Enter NURSE]

Go waken Juliet, go and trim her up. [11]
I'll go and chat with Paris. Hie, make haste,
Make haste. The bridegroom he is come already.
Make haste, I say.

[Exit CAPULET]

---

10. **straight.** straightway, immediately
11. **trim.** dress

Synopsis of Act IV, Scene 4

Early in the morning Wednesday, the Capulet household was busily preparing for the wedding feast. The Capulets and their servants were joking and happy. When Capulet heard music, he announced that Paris had arrived and told the Nurse to awaken Juliet.

Juxtaposition to Juliet's scene Shows the haste + impulsiveness Lighten the mood

---◆---

Before You Read Act IV, Scene 5

The humor of Scene 4 continues into the beginning of this one. Notice what a sharp contrast this produces. Soon the Nurse and the Capulets will find that Juliet is apparently dead. You will recall that both Capulet and Lady Capulet had previously wished angrily that "death is my son-in-law" and Juliet be "wedded to her grave." Now they discover that their angry statements seem to have come true. Note the lines in which Capulet describes how Juliet looks dead.

Notice the Friar offers consolation that is typical of a holy man in this circumstance. He is acting, but remember that his purposes are good. He hopes that the marriage of Romeo and Juliet will stop the age-old feud between the Capulets and the Montagues.

Notice that the tone of the scene changes again at the end. Why do you think that Shakespeare ended this act with a comic scene?

---◆---

ACT IV. Scene 5.

Location: Scene continues. Juliet's bed remains visible.

[*The* NURSE *goes to the bed*]

NURSE.
    Mistress! What, mistress! Juliet! Fast, I warrant
      her, she. [1]
    Why, lamb, why, lady! Fie, you slugabed! [2]
    Why, love, I say! Madam! Sweetheart! Why, bride!
    What, not a word? You take your pennyworths now. [3]
    Sleep for a week; for the next night, I warrant,
    The County Paris hath set up his rest [4]
    That you shall rest but little. God forgive me,
    Marry, and amen! How sound is she asleep!
    I needs must wake her. Madam, madam, madam!
    Ay, let the County take you in your bed;
    He'll fright you up, i' faith. Will it not be?
                [*She opens the bedcurtains*]
    What, dressed, and in your clothes, and down again? [5]
    I must needs wake you. Lady, lady, lady!
    Alas, alas! Help, help! My lady's dead!
    O, weraday, that ever I was born! [6]
    Some aqua vitae, ho! My lord! My lady! [7]

[*Enter* CAPULET'S WIFE]

---

1. **Fast.** fast asleep
2. **slugabed.** sleepyhead
3. **pennyworths.** small portions
4. **set up his rest.** firmly resolved
5. **down.** back in bed
6. **weraday.** wellaway, alas
7. **aqua vitae.** strong alcoholic spirits

WIFE.
What noise is here?

NURSE.
                    O lamentable day!

WIFE.
What is the matter?

NURSE.
                    Look, look! O heavy day! [8]

WIFE.
O me, O me! My child, my only life!
Revive, look up, or I will die with thee!
Help, help! Call help.

*didn't have a
good relationship
in the beginning*

[*Enter Father* CAPULET]

CAPULET.
For shame, bring Juliet forth. Her lord is come.

NURSE.
She's dead, deceased. She's dead, alack the day!

WIFE.
Alack the day, she's dead, she's dead, she's dead!

CAPULET.
Ha! Let me see her. Out, alas! She's cold.
Her blood is settled, and her joints are stiff; [9]
Life and these lips have long been separated.
Death lies on her like an untimely frost
Upon the sweetest flower of all the field.

---

8. **heavy.** sorrowful
9. **settled.** congealed, coagulated

NURSE.

O lamentable day!

WIFE.

O woeful time!

CAPULET.

Death, that hath ta'en her hence to make me wail,
Ties up my tongue and will not let me speak.

[*Enter* FRIAR LAURENCE *and the* COUNTY
PARIS, *with* MUSICIANS]

FRIAR LAURENCE.

Come, is the bride ready to go to church?

CAPULET.

Ready to go, but never to return.
O son, the night before thy wedding day
Hath Death lain with thy wife. There she lies,
Flower as she was, deflowered by him.
Death is my son-in-law, Death is my heir;
My daughter he hath wedded. I will die
And leave him all; life, living, all is Death's. [10]

PARIS.

Have I thought long to see this morning's face, [11]
And doth it give me such a sight as this?

WIFE.

Accurst, unhappy, wretched, hateful day! [12]
Most miserable hour that e'er time saw

---

10. **living.** means of making a living, property
11. **thought long.** looked forward to
12. **unhappy.** fatal

In lasting labor of his pilgrimage! [13]
But one, poor one, one poor and loving child,
But one thing to rejoice and solace in, [14]
And cruel Death hath catched it from my sight! [15]

NURSE.
O woe! O woeful, woeful, woeful day!
Most lamentable day, most woeful day
That ever, ever I did yet behold!
O day, O day, O day! O hateful day!
Never was seen so black a day as this.
O woeful day, O woeful day!

PARIS.
Beguiled, divorcèd, wrongèd, spited, slain! [16]
Most detestable Death, by thee beguiled,
By cruel, cruel thee quite overthrown!
O love! O life! Not life, but love in death!

CAPULET.
Despised, distressèd, hated, martyred, killed!
Uncomfortable time, why cam'st thou now [17]
To murder, murder our solemnity? [18]
O child! O child! My soul, and not my child!
Dead art thou! Alack, my child is dead,
And with my child my joys are burièd.

his life revolved around Juliet

---

13. **lasting.** unceasing, continuous
14. **solace.** find comfort
15. **catched.** snatched
16. **Beguiled.** cheated
17. **Uncomfortable.** painful, upsetting
18. **solemnity.** ceremony, festivity

FRIAR LAURENCE.
Peace, ho, for shame! Confusion's cure lives not [19]
In these confusions. Heaven and yourself
Had part in this fair maid; now heaven hath all,
And all the better is it for the maid.
Your part in her you could not keep from death, [20]
But heaven keeps his part in eternal life.
The most you sought was her promotion, [21]
For 'twas your heaven she should be advanced; [22]
And weep ye now, seeing she is advanced
Above the clouds, as high as heaven itself?
O, in this love you love your child so ill
That you run mad, seeing that she is well. [23]
She's not well married that lives married long,
But she's best married that dies married young.
Dry up your tears, and stick your rosemary [24]
On this fair corpse, and, as the custom is,
And in her best array, bear her to church;
For though fond nature bids us all lament, [25]
Yet nature's tears are reason's merriment. [26]

CAPULET.
All things that we ordainèd festival [27]

---

19. **Confusion's.** calamity's
20. **Your part.** the mortal part
21. **promotion.** social advancement
22. **your heaven.** your idea of the greatest good
23. **well.** blessed in heaven
24. **rosemary.** symbol of immortality and enduring love; therefore used at both funerals and weddings
25. **fond nature.** foolish human nature
26. **nature's ... merriment.** That which causes human nature to weep is an occasion of joy to reason.
27. **ordained festival.** intended to be part of a celebration

Turn from their office to black funeral: [28]
Our instruments to melancholy bells,
Our wedding cheer to a sad burial feast,
Our solemn hymns to sullen dirges change, [29]
Our bridal flowers serve for a buried corpse,
And all things change them to the contrary. [30]

FRIAR LAURENCE.
Sir, go you in, and, madam, go with him,
And go, Sir Paris. Everyone prepare
To follow this fair corpse unto her grave.
The heavens do lour upon you for some ill; [31]
Move them no more by crossing their high will. [32]

    [Exit. NURSE *and* MUSICIANS *remain]*

FIRST MUSICIAN.
Faith, we may put up our pipes and be gone.

NURSE.
Honest good fellows, ah, put up, put up!
For well you know this is a pitiful case.

                [Exit]

FIRST MUSICIAN.
Ay, by my troth, the case may be amended. [33]

[Enter PETER]

---

28. office. function
29. sullen. mournful   **dirges.** funeral hymns
30. them. themselves
31. lour. threaten, frown.   **for some ill.** on account of some sin
32. Move. anger
33. case ... amended. things generally could be much better;
the instrument case could be repaired

PETER.
Musicians, O, musicians, "Heart's ease," [34] "Heart's ease." O, an you will have me live, play "Heart's ease."

FIRST MUSICIAN.
Why "Heart's ease"?

PETER.
O, musicians, because my heart itself plays "My heart is full." O, play me some merry dump [35] to comfort me.

oxymoron

FIRST MUSICIAN.
Not a dump we! 'Tis no time to play now.

PETER.
You will not, then?

FIRST MUSICIAN.
No.

PETER.
I will then give it you soundly.

FIRST MUSICIAN.
What will you give us?

PETER.
No money, on my faith, but the gleek; [36] I will give you the minstrel. [37]

---

34. "Heart's ease," "My heart is full". popular ballads
35. dump. mournful tune or dance
36. gleek. jest, wisecrack
37. give you the minstrel. insultingly call you a minstrel, that is, a vagabond

FIRST MUSICIAN.

Then will I give you the serving-creature.

PETER.

Then will I lay the serving-creature's dagger on your pate. I will carry no crotchets. [38] I'll re you, I'll fa you. [39] Do you note [40] me?

FIRST MUSICIAN.

An you re us and fa us, you note us.

SECOND MUSICIAN.

Pray you, put up your dagger and put out your wit. [41]

PETER.

Then have at you with my wit! I will dry-beat [42] you with an iron wit, and put up my iron dagger. Answer me like men:

> "When griping griefs the heart doth wound,
> And doleful dumps the mind oppress,
> Then music with her silver sound" —

Why "silver sound"? Why "music with her silver sound"? What say you, Simon Catling? [43]

FIRST MUSICIAN.

Marry, sir, because silver hath a sweet sound.

---

38. **carry no crotchets.** stand for no whims; sing no quarter notes
39. **re, fa.** musical notes
40. **note.** listen to, set to music
41. **put out.** display
42. **dry-beat.** thrash without drawing blood
43. **Catling.** a small string made of catgut for a lute

PETER.
Pretty! what say you, Hugh Rebeck? [44]

SECOND MUSICIAN.
I say "silver sound" because musicians sound [45] for silver.

PETER.
Pretty too! What say you, James Soundpost? [46]

THIRD MUSICIAN.
Faith, I know not what to say.

PETER.
O, I cry you mercy, [47] you are the singer. I will say for you. It is "music with her silver sound" because musicians have no gold for sounding: [48]
 "Then music with her silver sound
 With speedy help doth lend redress."

           [Exit]

FIRST MUSICIAN.
What a pestilent knave is this same!

SECOND MUSICIAN.
Hang him, Jack! Come, we'll in here, tarry for the mourners, and stay [49] dinner.

           [Exit]

---

44. **Rebeck.** a fiddle with three strings
45. **sound.** play music
46. **Soundpost.** pillar or peg that supports the sounding board of a stringed instrument
47. **cry you mercy.** beg your pardon
48. **have ... sounding.** are paid only silver for playing
49. **stay.** wait for

Synopsis of Act IV, Scene 5

The morning of the wedding, the Nurse came to awaken Juliet, only to find her apparently dead. She called for help. Lady Capulet came, soon followed by her husband. Paris and the Friar entered shortly after. They all grieved over Juliet's death. Then the Friar stopped them by reminding them that Juliet was in heaven. They must accept God's will. Capulet ordered the wedding feast be turned into funeral preparations. Meanwhile, the musicians came in and there was a brief, comic scene between the musicians and Peter.

———————◆———————

Before You Read Act V, Scene 1

There is a great deal to look for in this short scene. It begins with more irony. Romeo is joyful in exile but it seems that he should be sad. Notice that the dream that has made him happy is just the opposite of what the Friar planned to happen. Shakespeare intended us to feel the chilling effect of Romeo's joyous but incorrect interpretation of his dream about death. Throughout this scene, notice that Romeo continues to use the image of light that he has used previously as he speaks about Juliet.

Be aware that Balthasar and the Friar act similarly in this scene. How do they both behave when speaking about Juliet's death?

The major themes of the play become very clear in Scene 1. The theme of fate is stressed here. Notice that Romeo feels that fate brought the lovers together and now fate has apparently separated them. He will not be separated from Juliet so he will join her in death. Note the change in Romeo. Remember that haste and impulsiveness have also been a theme of Shakespeare's.

Notice how Romeo's description of the apothecary and Juliet's soliloquy are similar. Both lovers turn to a potion for a solution to their predicament.

———————◆———————

ACT V. Scene 1.

Location: Mantua. A street.

[*Enter* ROMEO]

ROMEO.
    If I may trust the flattering truth of sleep, [1]
    My dreams presage some joyful news at hand. [2]
    My bosom's lord sits lightly in his throne, [3]
    And all this day an unaccustomed spirit
    Lifts me above the ground with cheerful thoughts.
    I dreamt my lady came and found me dead —
    Strange dream that gives a dead man leave to
       think! —
    And breathed such life with kisses in my lips
    That I revived and was an emperor.
    Ah me, how sweet is love itself possessed [4]
    When but love's shadows are so rich in joy! [5]

[*Enter* ROMEO'S *man* BALTHASAR, *booted*] [6]

    News from Verona! How now, Balthasar,
    Dost thou not bring me letters from the Friar?
    How doth my lady? Is my father well?
    How fares my Juliet? That I ask again,
    For nothing can be ill if she be well.

---

1. **flattering.** favorable; pleasing
2. **presage.** foretell
3. **bosom's lord.** heart
4. **itself possessed.** actually enjoyed
5. **shadows.** dreams
6. **booted.** wearing riding boots, indicating travel

BALTHASAR. *actually thinks she's dead*
Then she is well, and nothing can be ill.
Her body sleeps in Capels' monument, [7]
And her immortal part with angels lives.
I saw her laid low in her kindred's vault *she's dead*
And presently took post to tell it you. [8]
O, pardon me for bringing these ill news,
Since you did leave it for my office, sir. [9] *Dramatic Irony*

ROMEO.
Is it e'en so? Then I defy you, stars! *I defy fate*
Thou knowest my lodging. Get me ink and paper,
And hire post-horses. I will hence tonight.

BALTHASAR.
I do beseech you, sir, have patience.
Your looks are pale and wild, and do import [10]
Some misadventure. [11]

ROMEO.
              Tush, thou art deceived.
Leave me, and do the thing I bid thee do.
Hast thou no letters to me from the Friar?

BALTHASAR.
No, my good lord.

ROMEO.
              No matter. Get thee gone,
And hire those horses. I'll be with thee straight.

---

7. **Capels' monument.** burial vault of the Capulets
8. **presently took post.** immediately started off in haste
9. **office.** duty
10. **import.** suggest
11. **misadventure.** misfortune

[Exit BALTHASAR]

Well, Juliet, I will lie with thee tonight. *suicide*
Let's see for means. O mischief, thou art swift [12]
To enter in the thoughts of desperate men!
I do remember an apothecary — [13]
And hereabouts 'a dwells — which late I noted [14]
In tattered weeds, with overwhelming brows, [15]
Culling of simples. Meager were his looks; [16]
Sharp misery had worn him to the bones;
And in his needy shop a tortoise hung,
An alligator stuffed, and other skins
Of ill-shaped fishes; and about his shelves
A beggarly account of empty boxes, [17]
Green earthen pots, bladders, and musty seeds,
Remnants of packthread, and old cakes of roses [18]
Were thinly scattered to make up a show.
Noting this penury, to myself I said,
"An if a man did need a poison now, [19]
Whose sale is present death in Mantua, [20]
Here lives a caitiff wretch would sell it him." [21]

poss. earthy

---

12. **for means.** by what means
13. **apothecary.** druggist; maker and seller of drugs and
    medicines
14. **which ... noted.** whom I noticed recently
15. **weeds.** garments. **overwhelming brows.** eyebrows
    jutting out over his eyes
16. **simples.** medicinal herbs. **Meager.** poor, penniless
17. **beggarly account.** small number
18. **cakes of roses.** petals pressed into cakes to be used as
    perfume
19. **An if.** if
20. **present.** immediate
21. **caitiff.** miserable. **would.** who would

O, this same thought did but forerun my need,
And this same needy man must sell it me.
As I remember, this should be the house.
Being holiday, the beggar's shop is shut.
What, ho! Apothecary!

[*Enter* APOTHECARY]

APOTHECARY.

Who calls so loud?

ROMEO.

Come hither, man. I see that thou art poor.
Hold, there is forty ducats. [*He shows gold*] Let me have [22]
A dram of poison, such soon-speeding gear [23]
As will disperse itself through all the veins
That the life-weary taker may fall dead,
And that the trunk may be discharged of breath [24]
As violently as hasty powder fired
Doth hurry from the fatal cannon's womb.

APOTHECARY.

Such mortal drugs I have, but Mantua's law [25]
Is death to any he that utters them. [26]

ROMEO.

Art thou so bare and full of wretchedness,
And fearest to die? Famine is in thy cheeks,

---

22. ducats. gold coins
23. soon-speeding gear. fast-working stuff
24. trunk. body
25. mortal. deadly
26. any he. anyone.   **utters.** gives out, sells

Need and oppression starveth in thy eyes, [27]
Contempt and beggary hangs upon thy back.
The world is not thy friend, nor the world's law;
The world affords no law to make thee rich.
Then be not poor, but break it, and take this.

APOTHECARY.
My poverty but not my will consents. *only for the $*

ROMEO.
I pay thy poverty and not thy will.

APOTHECARY.
Put this in any liquid thing you will
And drink it off, and if you had the strength
Of twenty men it would dispatch you straight.

[*He gives poison, and takes the gold*]

ROMEO.
There is thy gold — worse poison to men's souls,
Doing more murder in this loathsome world
Than these poor compounds that thou mayst not
    sell. [28]
I sell thee poison; thou hast sold me none.
Farewell. Buy food, and get thyself in flesh. —
Come, cordial and not poison, go with me [29]
To Juliet's grave, for there must I use thee.

gold is poison (wants need)   [*Exit separately*]

---

27. **starveth.** are revealed by the starving look
28. **compounds.** mixtures
29. **cordial.** restorative for the heart

Synopsis of Act V, Scene 1

In Mantua, Romeo had a dream about death which he misinterpreted. He thought it was a happy omen, but he soon learned it was the opposite. His servant Balthasar arrived from Verona with news of Juliet's "death." Romeo decided to return to Verona where he planned to join Juliet in death. After sending Balthasar for horses, he persuaded a poor apothecary to sell him poison by offering the man an enormous sum of money. Romeo took the poison and left.

Before You Read Act V, Scene 2

Fate again interferes in the lives of the lovers. We learn why Friar Laurence was unable to notify Romeo of the plan. A plague and a subsequent quarantine prevented a messenger from reaching Romeo. Notice the role of death here. Now fate affects the Friar negatively. His statement, "Unhappy fortune," shows that he is only too aware that he is involved in a dangerous situation. Notice how these events have shattered his calm and philosophical nature.

ACT V. Scene 2.

Location: Verona. Friar Laurence's cell.

[*Enter* FRIAR JOHN *to* FRIAR LAURENCE]

FRIAR JOHN.
Holy Franciscan friar! Brother, ho!

[*Enter* FRIAR LAURENCE]

FRIAR LAURENCE.
This same should be the voice of Friar John.
Welcome from Mantua! What says Romeo?
Or if his mind be writ, give me his letter. [1]

FRIAR JOHN.
Going to find a barefoot brother out —
One of our order — to associate me [2]
Here in this city visiting the sick,
And finding him, the searchers of the town, [3]
Suspecting that we both were in a house
Where the infectious pestilence did reign,
Sealed up the doors and would not let us forth,
So that my speed to Mantua there was stayed. [4]

FRIAR LAURENCE.
Who bare my letter, then, to Romeo?

FRIAR JOHN.
I could not send it — here it is again —

---

1. **mind.** thoughts
2. **associate.** accompany
3. **searchers of the town.** town health officials who
   search for victims of the pestilence or plague
4. **speed.** successful journey, progress. **stayed.** prevented

Nor get a messenger to bring it thee,
So fearful were they of infection.

[*He gives a letter*]

FRIAR LAURENCE.
Unhappy fortune! By my brotherhood,
The letter was not nice but full of charge, [5]
Of dear import, and the neglecting it [6]
May do much danger. Friar John, go hence.
Get me an iron crow and bring it straight [7]
Unto my cell.

FRIAR JOHN.
Brother, I'll go and bring it thee.

[*Exit*]

FRIAR LAURENCE.
Now must I to the monument alone.
Within this three hours will fair Juliet wake.
She will beshrew me much that Romeo [8]
Hath had no notice of these accidents; [9]
But I will write again to Mantua,
And keep her at my cell till Romeo come —
Poor living corpse, closed in a dead man's tomb!

[*Exit*]

---

5. **nice.** trivial. **charge.** importance
6. **dear.** urgent, valuable
7. **crow.** crowbar
8. **beshrew.** reprove, blame
9. **accidents.** events

---◆---

Synopsis of Act V, Scene 2

Friar John, Friar Laurence's messenger, was unable to reach Romeo. The letter telling Romeo that Juliet was not really dead did not reach him. Friar John had been quarantined in Verona because of the plague. Laurence hurried to the Capulet tomb to reach Juliet since she was to awaken soon.

---◆---

---◆---

Before You Read Act V, Scene 3

This final scene takes place at night. Recall that other important scenes in the play also have taken place at night. Darkness and light have been important imagery throughout the play. Both lovers have used it to describe the moment, their love, or one another.

In this scene, Romeo and Juliet are about to be together again. Notice, though, they are not reunited in a way that anyone intended. However, Juliet receives another visitor. In the darkness, Romeo and this visitor fight, but neither knows the whole truth about his opponent.

The role of fate in this tragedy is very important here. Notice that Romeo tries to avenge himself against fate by his actions. The Friar actually is saved by fate. What he hoped to happen, the end of the feud, is accomplished. However, the peace that Father Laurence so desired is bought at a great price. Notice that this twist of fate calls to mind the Friar's earlier thought about good and evil being two sides of the same coin.

So the tragedy ends. The price of peace was very high. Notice that the injustice of the lovers' sacrifice must be judged against the conclusion of the ancient, bloody feud. There is, of course, irony because Romeo's and Juliet's deaths have guaranteed their eternal love.

---◆---

ACT V. Scene 3.

Location: Verona. A churchyard and the vault or tomb belonging to the Capulets.

[*Enter* PARIS, *and his* PAGE, *bearing flowers, perfumed water, and a torch*]

PARIS.
Give me thy torch, boy. Hence, and stand aloof. [1]
Yet put it out, for I would not be seen.
Under yond yew trees lay thee all along, [2]
Holding thy ear close to the hollow ground.
So shall no foot upon the churchyard tread,
Being loose, unfirm, with digging up of graves, [3]
But thou shalt hear it. Whistle then to me
As signal that thou hearest something approach.
Give me those flowers. Do as I bid thee. Go.

PAGE.
    [*Aside*]
I am almost afraid to stand alone
Here in the churchyard, yet I will adventure. [4]

                              [*He retires*]

PARIS.
          [*Strewing flowers and perfumed water*]
Sweet flower, with flowers thy bridal bed I strew — [5]

---

1. **aloof.** aside, at a distance
2. **all along.** at full length, flat
3. **Being.** the soil being
4. **adventure.** chance it
5. **Sweet.** perfumed

O woe! Thy canopy is dust and stones — [6]
Which with sweet water nightly I will dew, [7]
   Or wanting that, with tears distilled by moans. [8]
The obsequies that I for thee will keep [9]
Nightly shall be to strew thy grave and weep.

> [*Whistle* BOY]

The boy gives warning something doth approach.
What cursèd foot wanders this way tonight,
To cross my obsequies and true love's rite? [10]
What, with a torch? Muffle me, night, awhile. [11]

> [*He retires*]

[*Enter* ROMEO *and* BALTHASAR, *with a torch, a mattock, and a crowbar*] [12]

ROMEO.
Give me that mattock and the wrenching iron. [13]

> [*He takes the tools*] *suicide note*

Hold, take this letter. Early in the morning
See thou deliver it to my lord and father.

> [*He gives a letter and takes a torch*]

Give me the light. Upon thy life I charge thee,

---

6. **canopy.** covering
7. **dew.** moisten
8. **wanting.** lacking
9. **obsequies.** ceremonies in memory of the dead
10. **cross.** interrupt
11. **Muffle.** conceal
12. **mattock.** pickax
13. **wrenching iron.** crowbar

Whate'er thou hearest or seest, stand all aloof
And do not interrupt me in my course. [14]
Why I descend into this bed of death
Is partly to behold my lady's face,
But chiefly to take thence from her dead finger
A precious ring—a ring that I must use
In dear employment. Therefore hence, begone. [15]
But if thou, jealous, dost return to pry [16]
In what I farther shall intend to do,
By heaven, I will tear thee joint by joint
And strew this hungry churchyard with thy limbs.
The time and my intents are savage-wild,
More fierce and more inexorable far [17]
Than empty tigers or the roaring sea. [18]

BALTHASAR.
I will be gone, sir, and not trouble ye.

ROMEO.
So shalt thou show me friendship. Take thou that.

[*He gives him money*]

Live, and be prosperous; and farewell, good fellow.

BALTHASAR.
[*Aside*]
For all this same, I'll hide me hereabout. [19]
His looks I fear, and his intents I doubt. [20]

---

14. course. intended action
15. dear employment. important business
16. jealous. suspicious
17. inexorable. uncontrollable
18. empty. hungry
19. For all this same. all the same
20. doubt. suspect

[He retires]

ROMEO.
Thou detestable maw, thou womb of death, [21]
Gorged with the dearest morsel of the earth,
Thus I enforce thy rotten jaws to open,
And in despite I'll cram thee with more food. [22]

[He begins to open the tomb]

PARIS.
This is that banished haughty Montague
That murdered my love's cousin, with which grief
It is supposèd the fair creature died,
And here is come to do some villainous shame
To the dead bodies. I will apprehend him. [23]

[He comes forward]

Stop thy unhallowed toil, vile Montague!
Can vengeance be pursued further than death?
Condemnèd villain, I do apprehend thee.
Obey and go with me, for thou must die.

ROMEO.
I must indeed, and therefore came I hither.
Good gentle youth, tempt not a desperate man.
Fly hence and leave me. Think upon these gone; [24]
Let them affright thee. I beseech thee, youth,
Put not another sin upon my head
By urging me to fury. O, begone!

---

21. **maw.** mouth. **womb.** belly
22. **in despite.** defiantly, in scorn
23. **apprehend.** arrest
24. **gone.** dead

By heaven, I love thee better than myself.
For I come hither armed against myself.
Stay not, begone. Live, and hereafter say
A madman's mercy bid thee run away.

PARIS.
I do defy thy conjuration, [25]
And apprehend thee for a felon here. [26]

ROMEO.
Wilt thou provoke me? Then have at thee, boy!

[They fight]

PAGE.
O Lord, they fight! I will go call the watch.

[Exit]

PARIS
O, I am slain! *[He falls]* If thou be merciful,
Open the tomb, lay me with Juliet.

[He dies]

ROMEO.
In faith, I will. Let me peruse this face. [27]
Mercutio's kinsman, noble County Paris!
What said my man when my betossèd soul [28]
Did not attend him as we rode? I think [29]
He told me Paris should have married Juliet.
Said he not so? Or did I dream it so?
Or am I mad, hearing him talk of Juliet,

---

25. conjuration. solemn appeal
26. felon. criminal
27. peruse. look at
28. betossèd. upset
29. attend. pay attention to

To think it was so? O, give me thy hand,
One writ with me in sour misfortune's book.
I'll bury thee in a triumphant grave.

[*He opens the tomb*]

A grave? O, no! A lantern, slaughtered youth, [30]
For here lies Juliet, and her beauty makes
This vault a feasting presence full of light. [31]
Death, lie thou there, by a dead man interred.

[*He lays* PARIS *in the tomb*]

How oft when men are at the point of death
Have they been merry, which their keepers call [32]
A lightening before death! O, how may I [33]
Call this a lightening? O my love, my wife!
Death, that hath sucked the honey of thy breath,
Hath had no power yet upon thy beauty.
Thou art not conquered; beauty's ensign yet [34]
Is crimson in thy lips and in thy cheeks,
And death's pale flag is not advancèd there. [35]
Tybalt, liest thou there in thy bloody sheet? [36]
O, what more favor can I do to thee
Than with that hand that cut thy youth in twain
To sunder his that was thine enemy? [37]
Forgive me, cousin! Ah, dear Juliet,
Why art thou yet so fair? Shall I believe

---

30. lantern. turret room full of windows
31. feasting presence. reception chamber for feasting
32. keepers. attendants
33. lightening. exhilaration
34. ensign. banner
35. advancèd. raised
36. sheet. shroud
37. sunder. cut off. **his.** my (Romeo's) own

That unsubstantial Death is amorous, [38]
And that the lean abhorrèd monster keeps
Thee here in dark to be his paramour?
For fear of that I still will stay with thee [39]
And never from this palace of dim night
Depart again. Here, here will I remain
With worms that are thy chambermaids. O, here
Will I set up my everlasting rest
And shake the yoke of inauspicious stars [40]
From this world-wearied flesh. Eyes, look your last!
Arms, take your last embrace! And, lips, O you
The doors of breath, seal with a righteous kiss
A dateless bargain to engrossing death! [41]
                              [He kisses JULIET]
Come, bitter conduct, come, unsavory guide, [42]
Thou desperate pilot, now at once run on [43]
The dashing rocks thy seasick weary bark!
Here's to my love. [He drinks] O true apothecary!
Thy drugs are quick. Thus with a kiss I die.
                              [He dies]

[Enter at the other end of the churchyard FRIAR
LAURENCE, with lantern, crow, and spade]

---

38. unsubstantial. lacking material existence
    amorous. full of love
39. still. always
40. inauspicious. promising misfortune
41. dateless bargain. everlasting contract. **engrossing.**
    monopolizing, taking all; also, drawing up the contract
42. conduct. guide (i.e., the poison)
43. desperate. reckless, despairing. **pilot.** captain

FRIAR LAURENCE.
Saint Francis be my speed! How oft tonight [44]
Have my old feet stumbled at graves! Who's there? [45]

BALTHASAR.
Here's one, a friend, and one that knows you well.

FRIAR LAURENCE.
Bliss be upon you. Tell me, good my friend,
What torch is yond that vainly lends his light [46]
To grubs and eyeless skulls? As I discern, [47]
It burneth in the Capels' monument.

BALTHASAR.
It doth so, holy sir, and there's my master,
One that you love.

FRIAR LAURENCE.
                    Who is it?

BALTHASAR.
                              Romeo.

FRIAR LAURENCE.
How long hath he been there?

BALTHASAR.
                              Full half an hour.

FRIAR LAURENCE.
Go with me to the vault.

---

44. be my speed. prosper me
45. stumbled. stumbling was bad luck
46. vainly. uselessly
47. grubs. insect larvae

BALTHASAR.

I dare not, sir.
My master knows not but I am gone hence,
And fearfully did menace me with death
If I did stay to look on his intents.

FRIAR LAURENCE.

Stay, then, I'll go alone. Fear comes upon me.
O, much I fear some ill unthrifty thing. [48]

BALTHASAR.

As I did sleep under this yew tree here
I dreamt my master and another fought,
And that my master slew him.

FRIAR LAURENCE.

[*Advancing to the tomb*] Romeo!
Alack, alack, what blood is this which stains
The stony entrance of this sepulcher?
What mean these masterless and gory swords [49]
To lie discolored by this place of peace?

[*He enters the tomb*]

Romeo! O, pale! Who else? What, Paris too?
And steeped in blood? Ah, what an unkind hour [50]
Is guilty of this lamentable chance!
The lady stirs.

[JULIET *wakes*]

---

48. **unthrifty.** unfortunate
49. **masterless.** discarded
50. **unkind.** unnatural

JULIET.
O comfortable Friar, where is my lord? [51]
I do remember well where I should be,
And there I am. Where is my Romeo?

[*A noise within*]

FRIAR LAURENCE.
I hear some noise. Lady, come from that nest
Of death, contagion, and unnatural sleep.
A greater power than we can contradict
Hath thwarted our intents. Come, come away.
Thy husband in thy bosom there lies dead,
And Paris, too. Come, I'll dispose of thee
Among a sisterhood of holy nuns.
Stay not to question, for the watch is coming.
Come, go, good Juliet. [*A noise again*] I dare no
   longer stay.

[*Exit* FRIAR LAURENCE]

JULIET.
Go, get thee hence, for I will not away.
What's here? A cup, closed in my true love's hand?
Poison, I see, hath been his timeless end. [52]
O churl, drunk all, and left no friendly drop [53]
To help me after? I will kiss thy lips;
Haply some poison yet doth hang on them, [54]
To make me die with a restorative. [55]

[*She kisses him*]

---

51. comfortable. comforting
52. timeless. untimely; everlasting
53. churl. miser
54. Haply. perhaps
55. restorative. medicine

Thy lips are warm.

[*Enter* PARIS'S BOY *and watch, at the other end of the churchyard*]

FIRST WATCH.
Lead, boy. Which way?

JULIET.
Yea, noise? Then I'll be brief. O happy dagger! [56]

[*She takes* ROMEO'S *dagger*]

This is thy sheath. There rust, and let me die.

[*She stabs herself and falls*]

PAGE.
This is the place, there where the torch doth burn.

FIRST WATCH.
The ground is bloody. Search about the churchyard.
Go, some of you, whoe'er you find attach. [57]

[*Exit some*]

Pitiful sight! Here lies the County slain,
And Juliet bleeding, warm, and newly dead,
Who here hath lain this two days burièd.
Go tell the Prince. Run to the Capulets.
Raise up the Montagues. Some others search.

[*Exit others*]

We see the ground whereon these woes do lie,

---

56. happy. timely, convenient
57. attach. arrest, detain

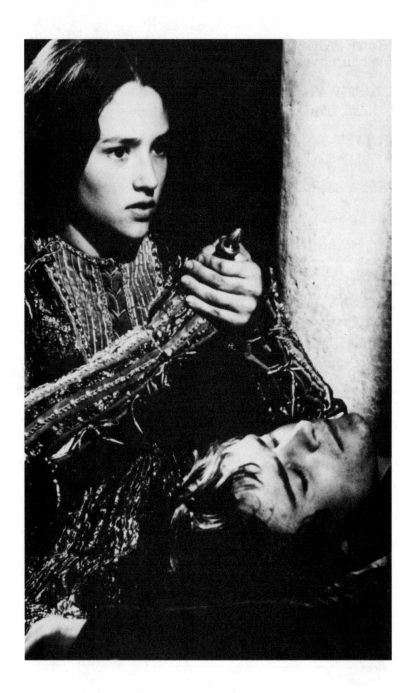

But the true ground of all these piteous woes [58]
We cannot without circumstance descry. [59]

[*Enter some of the watch, with* ROMEO'S *man*
BALTHASAR]

SECOND WATCH.
Here's Romeo's man. We found him in the churchyard.

FIRST WATCH.
Hold him in safety till the Prince come hither. [60]

[*Enter* FRIAR LAURENCE, *and another*
WATCHMAN *with tools*]

THIRD WATCH.
Here is a friar, that trembles, sighs, and weeps.
We took this mattock and this spade from him
As he was coming from this churchyard's side.

FIRST WATCH.
A great suspicion. Stay the Friar too. [61]

[*Enter the* PRINCE *and attendants*]

PRINCE.
What misadventure is so early up
That calls our person from our morning rest?

[*Enter* CAPELS (CAPULET *and* HIS WIFE)]

---

58. ground. cause
59. circumstance. details.   **descry.** uncover
60. in safety. under guard
61. Stay. detain

CAPULET.
What should it be that is so shrieked abroad?

CAPULET'S WIFE.
O, the people in the street cry "Romeo,"
Some "Juliet," and some "Paris," and all run
With open outcry toward our monument.

PRINCE.
What fear is this which startles in our ears? [62]

FIRST WATCH.
Sovereign, here lies the County Paris slain,
And Romeo dead, and Juliet, dead before,
Warm and new killed.

PRINCE.
Search, seek, and know how this foul murder
    comes. [63]

FIRST WATCH.
Here is a friar, and slaughtered Romeo's man,
With instruments upon them fit to open [64]
These dead men's tombs.

CAPULET.
O heavens! O wife, look how our daughter bleeds!
This dagger hath mista'en, for lo, his house [65]
Is empty on the back of Montague,
And it mis-sheathèd in my daughter's bosom!

---

62. startles. cries alarmingly
63. know. learn
64. instruments. tools
65. his house. its sheath

CAPULET'S WIFE.
O me! this sight of death is as a bell
That warns my old age to a sepulcher.

[*Enter* MONTAGUE]

PRINCE.
Come, Montague, for thou art early up
To see thy son and heir now early down.

MONTAGUE.
Alas, my liege, my wife is dead tonight; [66]
Grief of my son's exile hath stopped her breath.
What further woe conspires against mine age?

PRINCE.
Look, and thou shalt see.

MONTAGUE.
  [*Seeing* ROMEO'S *body*]
O thou untaught! What manners is in this, [67]
To press before thy father to a grave? [68]

PRINCE.
Seal up the mouth of outrage for a while, [69]
Till we can clear these ambiguities
And know their spring, their head, their true
    descent; [70]
And then will I be general of your woes [71]

---

66. liege. lord
67. untaught. ill-mannered youth
68. press. hurry, go
69. outrage. outcry
70. spring, head. source
71. be ... woes. be leader in mourning

And lead you even to death. Meantime forbear, [72]
And let mischance be slave to patience. [73]
Bring forth the parties of suspicion. [74]

FRIAR LAURENCE.
I am the greatest, able to do least,
Yet most suspected, as the time and place
Doth make against me, of this direful murder; [75]
And here I stand, both to impeach and purge [76]
Myself condemnèd and myself excused.

PRINCE. _calmest_
Then say at once what thou dost know in this.

FRIAR LAURENCE.
I will be brief, for my short date of breath [77]
Is not so long as is a tedious tale.
Romeo, there dead, was husband to that Juliet,
And she, there dead, that Romeo's faithful wife.
I married them, and their stol'n marriage day
Was Tybalt's doomsday, whose untimely death
Banished the new-made bridegroom from this city,
For whom, and not for Tybalt, Juliet pined.
You, to remove that siege of grief from her,
Betrothed and would have married her perforce [78]
To County Paris. Then comes she to me,

---

72. **to death.** as far as the dead bodies
73. **let ... patience.** be patient in our misfortune
74. **of.** under
75. **make.** conspire, tell. **direful.** terrible
76. **to impeach.** to accuse. **purge.** declare blameless
77. **date of breath.** time left to live
78. **perforce.** by compulsion

And with wild looks bid me devise some means
To rid her from this second marriage,
Or in my cell there would she kill herself.
Then gave I her — so tutored by my art —
A sleeping potion, which so took effect
As I intended, for it wrought on her [79]
The form of death. Meantime I writ to Romeo [80]
That he should hither come as this dire night [81]
To help to take her from her borrowed grave,
Being the time the portion's force should cease.
But he which bore my letter, Friar John,
Was stayed by accident, and yesternight [82]
Returned my letter back. Then all alone
At the prefixèd hour of her waking
Came I to take her from her kindred's vault,
Meaning to keep her closely at my cell [83]
Till I conveniently could send to Romeo.
But when I came, some minute ere the time
Of her awakening, here untimely lay
The noble Paris and true Romeo dead.
She wakes, and I entreated her come forth
And bear this work of heaven with patience.
But then a noise did scare me from the tomb,
And she, too desperate, would not go with me,
But, as it seems, did violence on herself.
All this I know, and to the marriage
Her nurse is privy; and if aught in this [84]

---

79. wrought. fashioned, created
80. form. appearance
81. as this. this very
82. stayed. stopped
83. closely. secretly
84. privy. in on the secret

Miscarried by my fault, let my old life
Be sacrificed some hour before his time [85]
Unto the rigor of severest law. [86]

guilty - if it's my 85 fault, do whatever

PRINCE.
We still have known thee for a holy man. [87]
Where's Romeo's man? What can he say to this?

BALTHASAR.
I brought my master news of Juliet's death,
And then in post he came from Mantua [88]
To this same place, to this same monument.
This letter he early bid me give his father, [89]
[Showing a letter]
And threatened me with death, going in the vault,
If I departed not and left him there.

PRINCE.
[Taking the letter]
Give me the letter. I will look on it.
Where is the County's page, that raised the watch?
Sirrah, what made your master in this place? [90]

PAGE.
He came with flowers to strew his lady's grave,
And bid me stand aloof, and so I did.
Anon comes one with light to ope the tomb,
And by and by my master drew on him,
And then I ran away to call the watch.

---

85. his. its
86. rigor. strictness
87. still. always
88. post. haste
89. early. early in the morning
90. made. did

PRINCE.

This letter doth make good the Friar's words,
Their course of love, the tidings of her death;
And here he writes that he did buy a poison
Of a poor 'pothecary, and therewithal [91]
Came to this vault to die, and lie with Juliet.
Where be these enemies? Capulet, Montague,
See what a scourge is laid upon your hate,
That heaven finds means to kill your joys with
    love. [92]
And I, for winking at your discords, too [93]
Have lost a brace of kinsmen. All are punished. [94]

CAPULET.

O brother Montague, give me thy hand.
This is my daughter's jointure, for no more [95]
Can I demand.

MONTAGUE.

        But I can give thee more,
For I will raise her statue in pure gold,
That whiles Verona by that name is known
There shall no figure at such rate be set [96]
As that of true and faithful Juliet.

---

91. **therewithal.** with the poison
92. **kill your joys.** destroy your happiness; kill your
    children. **with.** by means of
93. **winking at.** shutting my eyes to
94. **a brace of.** two
95. **jointure.** marriage portion
96. **rate.** value

CAPULET.

As rich shall Romeo's by his lady's lie;
Poor sacrifices of our enmity! [97]

PRINCE.

A glooming peace this morning with it brings; [98]
The sun, for sorrow, will not show his head.
Go hence to have more talk of these sad things.
Some shall be pardoned, and some punished;
For never was a story of more woe
Than this of Juliet and her Romeo.

[*Exit*]

In Shakespeare, if the characters come to recognize their blindness, the play is a comedy; that is, it has a basically happy ending. However, if the characters continue their blindness, the play becomes a tragedy.

---

97. **enmity.** hostility
98. **glooming.** cloudy, gloomy

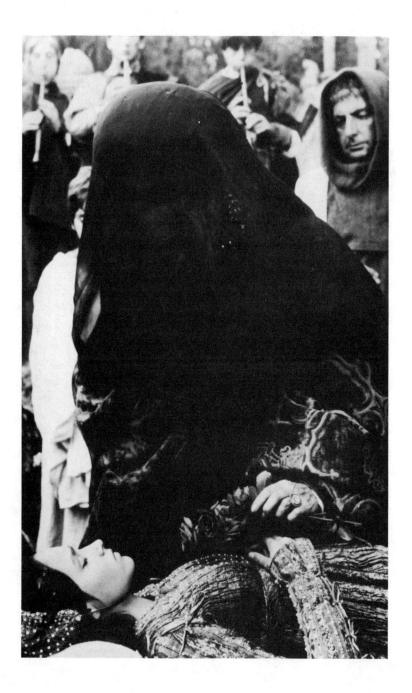

Synopsis of Act V, Scene 3

As the scene opened, Paris was mourning the death of Juliet. His servant warned him that someone was coming. Paris hid, but watched to see who came.

It was Romeo, of course, with his servant Balthasar. They had brought tools to break into the tomb. Romeo pretended that he simply wanted to look once more at Juliet, and sent a letter with Balthasar to his father. The letter contained the truth about what had happened. The servant, however, feared that his master would do something rash: "His looks I fear, and his intents I doubt," so he stayed by the tomb.

Paris, seeing Romeo opening the tomb, thought that he was going to vandalize the Capulet tomb. The two fought, and Paris was killed. When Romeo realized whom he had killed, he granted Paris's request to be put by Juliet's side. Romeo saw Juliet's body and was struck again by her beauty. In a beautiful passage, he promised to remain with her forever. Romeo then drank the poison.

Friar Laurence arrived at this moment, just a moment too late. As he entered the tomb, he saw the bloody weapons and feared the worst. When Juliet awoke, asking for Romeo, he urged her to come with him. There was no time to be gentle. He had to tell her straight out that Romeo "...there lies dead." She refused to accompany him, and the Friar fled in fear. Juliet then tried to drink from the flask. When she found it empty, she stabbed herself with Romeo's dagger.

The Prince entered, followed by the Capulets
and Montague. Many questions were asked. The
Friar told all he knew. Romeo's letter and evidence
given by Balthasar and Paris's servant confirmed
the Friar's story. Friar Laurence courageously
offered his life, for he felt responsible for the
tragedy. The Prince recognized that the Friar was
not at fault. Instead he blamed the feuding families
and his own leniency. Capulet and Montague ended
their feud and promised to build a golden statue
to honor their children. The Prince closed the play
with this sad couplet: "For never was a story of
more woe/ Than this of Juliet and her Romeo."

REVIEWING

YOUR

READING

Act I, Scene 1

FINDING THE MAIN IDEA

1. The purpose of the Prologue is to
(A) introduce the chorus (B) show the audience that fate played a major role in the tragedy (C) give the audience a chance to find their seats (D) tell where the play takes place

2. The first scene introduces the feud between
(A) Romeo and Juliet (B) Gregory and Samson (C) the Montagues and the Capulets (D) Benvolio and Romeo

REMEMBERING DETAIL

3. When the Prince says "If ever you disturb our streets again,/Your lives shall pay the forfeit of the peace," he means that
(A) everyone will ignore them (B) the people fighting will be executed (C) the Prince will choose the winner (D) the people fighting will not be allowed onto the street anymore

4. Romeo is dejected because
(A) he is in love with Juliet, and Juliet is not in love with him (B) there has been a fight (C) he thinks the Prince is angry (D) he is in love with Rosaline, and Rosaline is not in love with him

5. Benvolio thinks that Romeo should
(A) immediately marry Rosaline (B) forget about Rosaline by looking at other women (C) persuade Tybalt to marry Rosaline (D) try to win Rosaline by giving her gifts

DRAWING CONCLUSIONS

6. You can guess that Benvolio
(A) often is the one who tries to make peace (B) usually starts the fights (C) has been wounded in a fight with the Capulets (D) is a spy for the Capulets

USING YOUR REASON

7. Judging by the way that Gregory and Samson speak, you can guess that they are
   (A) nobles (B) prophets (C) servants (D) priests
8. Romeo ran from Bevolio into the woods because
   (A) he was feeling sad and did not want to talk (B) he was hunting an animal in the woods (C) he was looking for Rosaline in the woods (D) he was angry at Benvolio

IDENTIFYING THE MOOD

9. When Benvolio hears that Romeo is in love with Rosaline, Benvolio is
   (A) angry (B) sad (C) amused (D) shocked

THINKING IT OVER

1. Do we ever find out what started the Montagues' and the Capulets' "ancient quarrel?" Does either house ever do anything to resolve the argument, or do they actually encourage the fighting? Do you think that either the Montagues or the Capulets have ever thought about possible consequences of their feud? Explain your answers.
2. Notice the language Romeo uses when describing his feelings for Rosaline. Do you think that Romeo is truly in love with Rosaline? What does Benvolio seem to think about Romeo's feelings for Rosaline? What does Benvolio's opinion tell you about Romeo's love for Rosaline? Explain your answer.

Act I, Scene 2

FINDING THE MAIN IDEA

1. The most important thing that happens in this act is that
   (A) Romeo and Benvolio decide to go to Capulet's party
   (B) Capulet tells his servant to invite people to the party
   (C) Capulet says he thinks he can live in peace with Montague (D) Benvolio tells Romeo to forget about Rosaline

REMEMBERING DETAIL

2. Capulet says that Juliet is
   (A) eighteen years old (B) twenty-one years old
   (C) fourteen years old (D) sixteen years old
3. Capulet says that he will allow Paris to marry Juliet if
   (A) Paris comes to Capulet's party that evening (B) Juliet
   wants to marry Paris (C) Tybalt doesn't mind (D) Paris
   does not fall in love with someone else first
4. Romeo wants to go to Capulet's party in order to
   (A) have an enjoyable evening of dancing (B) see Rosaline
   (C) keep Benvolio company (D) fight with Tybalt

DRAWING CONCLUSIONS

5. When the Servant says he "...can never find what names
   the writing person hath here writ," he means that he
   (A) has poor eyesight and cannot see the page (B) does not
   know how to read (C) always loses the paper he is supposed
   to read (D) can never find the people he has to visit

USING YOUR REASON

6. When the Servant says "come crush a cup of wine," he
   probably means
   (A) "come have a cup of wine with us" (B) "come squash
   a cup of wine" (C) "come help us make wine by stomp-
   ing on grapes" (D) "come and conquer the Capulets"
7. When Benvolio says "...I will make thee think thy swan a
   crow," he means that
   (A) Rosaline looks like a bird (B) Romeo will give up
   looking at women and take up bird watching (C) Romeo
   will be so in love with Rosaline that he will start seeing
   things that are not there (D) Rosaline will not look so
   attractive to Romeo after Romeo sees some other women
8. Why does Romeo say that he is "bound more than a madman is;/Shut up in prison, kept without my
   food,/Whipped and tormented..."?
   (A) He is a criminal on the run. (B) He is on a hunger
   strike that will end only when Rosaline notices him.
   (C) His father is punishing him. (D) He is suffering so
   much over Rosaline's ignoring him.

IDENTIFYING THE MOOD

9. Which of the following best describes the character of the Servant?
   (A) tragic (B) heroic (C) funny (D) bizarre

THINKING IT OVER

1. Compare the character of Paris with the character of Romeo. Do you think that Paris is more mature or less mature than Romeo? Why do you think so?
2. Based on his behavior in this scene, what kind of a person do you think Capulet is? Are his behavior and language consistent with what you have seen in Scene 1? What does this tell you about the quarrel between the Montagues and the Capulets?

ACT I, Scene 3

FINDING THE MAIN IDEA

1. The most important thing that happens in this act is that (A) The Nurse tells about her daughter Susan (B) Lady Capulet says that she was married very young (C) Lady Capulet asks if Juliet might like to marry Paris (D) the Nurse says that she likes Paris

REMEMBERING DETAIL

2. The Nurse describes Paris as a
   (A) "man of iron" (B) "man of steel" (C) "man of wax" (D) "man of clay"
3. Juliet says that she will look at Paris
   (A) only as much as her mother wants her to look
   (B) as much as she wants to look (C) as much as the nurse wants her to look (D) not at all

DRAWING CONCLUSIONS

4. You can assume that Juliet
   (A) doesn't know Paris very well (B) doesn't want to get married (C) prefers to marry Romeo (D) dislikes Paris

5. When the Nurse says that Paris is a "man of wax," she means that Paris

   (A) is very boring (B) has only one facial expression (C) is not very intelligent (D) is a model of a man

6. When Lady Capulet says "To beautify him only lacks a cover," she means that Paris

   (A) needs to wear more becoming clothes (B) needs only a wife to make him perfect (C) needs to work on improving his manners (D) needs to disguise himself so that women will leave him alone

7. When the Nurse says, "Nay, bigger! Women grow by men," she means that

   (A) Women are improved by being married (B) Women get taller when they get married (C) Women often get pregnant when they get married (D) A and C

IDENTIFYING THE MOOD

8. Lady Capulet's feelings toward Paris can be described as

   (A) romantic (B) admiring (C) disdainful (D) hateful

THINKING IT OVER

1. Juliet does not have many lines in this act. What do you think this says about her character so far? Do you think she will change as the play progresses? Why do you think so?

2. Compare the Nurse's language with Lady Capulet's. How is it different? Why do you think Shakespeare made the Nurse's language so different from Lady Capulet's?

ACT I, Scene 4

FINDING THE MAIN IDEA

1. This scene introduces the character of

   (A) Mercutio (B) Benvolio (C) Romeo (D) Rosaline

REMEMBERING DETAILS

2. Benvolio says that the group will

   (A) dance for a little while and then leave (B) cause a disturbance at the party (C) scare the women who are at the party (D) try and determine how big the room is

3. Mercutio tries to entertain Romeo with stories about
(A) Juliet (B) Queen Mab (C) foreign countries
(D) animals

DRAWING CONCLUSIONS
4. You can tell that Mercutio is a character who
(A) is very serious (B) has a biting sense of humor
(C) often starts fights (D) does not like Romeo

USING YOUR REASON
5. When Romeo says "But being heavy, I will bear the
light," he means
(A) he will carry the torch because he must lose weight
(B) he will carry the torch because he is bigger and
stronger than Mercutio (C) he is sad and he will carry the
torch (D) the torch is heavy but he will carry it anyway
6. When Mercutio says "And, to sink in it, should you burden love—..." he means
(A) if Romeo fell in love, Romeo would be a burden to
love (B) Romeo will probably never fall in love
(C) no one should ever fall in love (D) only a few people
should be in love at one time

IDENTIFYING THE MOOD
7. At the end of the scene, Romeo feels a sense of
(A) happiness (B) uneasiness (C) shock (D) sadness

THINKING IT OVER
1. Based upon what you have read in the scene, what type
of a character do you think Mercutio is? Is he a very serious character, or is he comical? What dramatic purpose
does he serve?
2. Reread Romeo's speech at the end of Scene 4. Why does
he have the kind of feeling he says he has? Do you think
there is any reason for him to have such a feeling? Why
do you think so?

Act I, Scene 5

FINDING THE MAIN IDEA

1. The most important thing that happens in this scene is
   (A) the servingmen get confused about the party
   (B) Capulet will not let Tybalt fight with Romeo
   (C) Romeo talks to the Nurse (D) Romeo and Juliet meet
   and fall in love with each other

REMEMBERING DETAILS

2. Tybalt wants to
   (A) welcome Romeo to the party (B) ignore Romeo
   (C) fight with Romeo (D) fight with the Servingman
3. When Capulet says, "'A bears him like a portly gentleman..." he means that
   (A) Romeo is fat (B) Romeo behaves like a dignified
   gentleman (C) Tybalt behaves like a dignified gentleman
   (D) the Servingman behaves like a dignifies gentleman
4. Juliet compares herself and Romeo to
   (A) a tree trunk and a leaf (B) a lip and a hand (C) a saint
   and a pilgrim (D) a book and a page

DRAWING CONCLUSIONS

5. You can assume that later in the play Tybalt will
   (A) become good friends with Romeo (B) propose mar-
   riage to Juliet (C) try to start another fight with Romeo
   (D) get sick and die

USING YOUR REASON

6. When Juliet says, "You kiss by th' book," she means that
   (A) Romeo kisses in an expert way (B) Romeo kisses
   only when he has permission (C) Romeo's lips feel like
   paper (D) Romeo is shy about kissing her
7. When Romeo says "My life is my foe's debt," he means
   that
   (A) the Montagues owe him some money (B) his life is at
   the mercy of the Montagues (C) he will pay the
   Montagues so they will allow him to marry Juliet (D) he
   thinks the Montagues will pay Tybalt to kill him

IDENTIFYING THE MOOD

8. At the end of the scene, Juliet feels
(A) dismayed (B) joyful (C) confused (D) jealous

THINKING IT OVER

1. Are Romeo's feelings for Juliet the same as his feelings for Rosaline? Why or why not? On what do you base your opinion?
2. In this scene, is there any change in Romeo's and Juliet's characters? Do they seem to act differently from the way they had acted in previous scenes? If so, how are they different?

ACT II, Scene 1

FINDING THE MAIN IDEA

1. Which line(s) best summarize Romeo's purpose in this scene?
   (A) "And on my life, hath stol'n him home to bed."
   (B) "Come, he hath hid himself among these trees/To be consorted with the humorous night./Blind is his love and best befits the dark." (C) "He ran this way and leapt this orchard wall." (D) "Go then, for 'tis in vain/To seek him here that means not to be found."

REMEMBERING DETAIL

2. The line, "By her high forehead and her scarlet lip," describes
   (A) Juliet (B) Rosaline (C) the Nurse (D) Lady Capulet
3. Mercutio jokes that he will find Romeo by
   (A) leaping the orchard wall (B) loudly calling out his name (C) reciting a spell to make him appear (D) searching for him among the trees

USING YOUR REASON

4. Mercutio's statement, "I conjure thee by Rosaline's bright eyes," shows that
   (A) Mercutio believes he has special powers
   (B) Mercutio believes Romeo still loves Rosaline
   (C) Mercutio is falling in love with Rosaline
   (D) Mercutio can make Romeo appear if he uses the right words

DRAWING CONCLUSIONS

5. You can conclude that Romeo
   (A) falls in love too easily (B) is madly in love with Juliet (C) is only infatuated with Juliet (D) will grow to love Juliet less

IDENTIFYING THE MOOD

6. This scene, from Mercutio's point of view, is
   (A) serious (B) mysterious (C) gloomy (D) humorous

1. It is ironic that Mercutio teases Romeo about his love for Rosaline. Why is this so?
2. What is Benvolio's role in this scene? Do you believe he is a better friend to Romeo than Mercutio is? Explain your answer.

ACT II, Scene 2

FINDING THE MAIN IDEA
1. The most important thing that happens in this scene is
   (A) Romeo and Juliet finally speak to another (B) Romeo and Juliet confess their love and vow to be married
   (C) Juliet expresses reservations about seeing Romeo
   (D) Romeo reveals his sensitive nature

REMEMBERING DETAIL
2. In which line does Juliet express her sorrow that Romeo is a Montague?
   (A) "I would not for the world they saw thee here."
   (B) "Bondage is hoarse and may not speak aloud,"
   (C) "Good night, good night! Parting is such sweet sorrow/That I shall say good night till it be morrow."
   (D) "O Romeo, Romeo! Wherefore art thou Romeo?"
3. What image does Juliet use to explain that Romeo's name is unimportant?
   (A) a glove (B) a river (C) the moon (D) a rose
4. At what time will Juliet send the Nurse for instructions from Romeo?
   (A) nine o'clock (B) twelve o'clock (C) six o'clock
   (D) one o'clock

DRAWING CONCLUSIONS
5. Shakespeare used rhymed couplets in this scene to
   (A) make the scene longer (B) emphasize the loving feelings between Romeo and Juliet (C) make it easier to memorize (D) contrast it to the previous scene

USING YOUR REASON
6. A betrothal is the same as
   (A) a wedding (B) an engagement (C) a honeymoon (D) love

7. Juliet's request, "O, swear not be the moon, th' inconstant moon," means she wants a love which is (A) brighter than the moon (B) stable, not fickle (C) subject to change (D) earthly and common

IDENTIFYING THE MOOD
8. The mood of this scene is (A) humorous (B) suspenseful (C) romantic (D) sad

THINKING IT OVER
1. Do you believe Romeo and Juliet are too hasty in their love? If it were you, would you handle the courtship differently? How would you handle it?
2. What changes are taking place in Juliet? Is she the same meek little girl as in Act I? Do you think Romeo changes, too? If so, how does he change?
3. Compare and contrast Romeo and Juliet as they confess their love. In your opinion, who is more impulsive? Who is more realistic? Give examples to support your opinions.

ACT II, Scene 3

FINDING THE MAIN IDEA
1. This main thing that happens in this scene is that Romeo asks the Friar (A) to prepare a love potion (B) to marry him and Juliet (C) what he thinks of Juliet (D) to pray for him

REMEMBERING DETAIL
2. The scene opens with the Friar talking to (A) himself (B) Romeo (C) Juliet (D) Holy Saint Francis
3. The Friar states that plants and flowers (A) are too beautiful to be picked (B) have souls just like people (C) are useless things (D) can heal or hurt
4. The line, "Holy Saint Francis! What a change is here!" refers to Romeo's feelings toward (A) the Friar (B) Juliet (C) Rosaline (D) the Capulets

DRAWING CONCLUSIONS

5. Because of Romeo's sudden loss of interest in Rosaline, you can figure that the Friar believes Romeo
(A) changes his mind too quickly (B) is correct to choose Juliet (C) should reconsider Rosaline (D) is ready to get married

USING YOUR REASON

6. The Friar's words, "For this alliance may so happy prove/To turn your households' rancor to pure love," shows that he believes marriage might
(A) destroy the two families (B) stop the feud (C) create more problems (D) be hard to avoid

7. Which line warns Romeo that a hasty marriage might lead to trouble?
(A) "Be plain, good son, and homely in thy drift."
(B) "Women may fall when there's no strength in men."
(C) "Wisely and slow. They stumble that run fast."
(D) "The gray-eyed morn smiles on the frowning night."

IDENTIFYING THE MOOD

8. The Friar's tone throughout this scene is
(A) sensible (B) frivolous (C) humorous (D) angry

THINKING IT OVER

1. Contrast Romeo and Friar Lawrence. In what ways are they different? In your opinion, which man thinks and behaves more logically? Explain your opinion.

2. Why do you believe Shakespeare bothered to describe the Friar's special talent with herbs? Predict how this special talent might affect the play's outcome.

ACT II, Scene 4

FINDING THE MAIN IDEA

1. The main purpose of this scene is to
(A) expose the plan Romeo has devised to wed Juliet
(B) inform the audience about fencing terminology
(C) introduce the Nurse (D) show Mercutio's teasing nature

2. Another major thing we learn in this scene is that
(A) the Nurse has a servant named Peter (B) Tybalt has

282

challenged Romeo to a duel (C) Mercutio makes fun of
the Nurse (D) the scene takes place in a square

REMEMBERING DETAIL

3. The news that Tybalt has challenged Romeo to a duel is
   written
   (A) in a public notice (B) in the local newspaper (C) in a
   letter (D) on a wall
4. The line, "Commend me to thy lady," is spoken three
   times by
   (A) Mercutio (B) Benvolio (C) Romeo (D) the Nurse
5. Romeo will send a "tackled stair." This is a
   (A) helper (B) rope ladder (C) bag of money (D) token of
   affection

DRAWING CONCLUSIONS

6. Mercutio and the Nurse
   (A) have low opinions of each other (B) think fondly of
   each other (C) are likely to fall in love (D) will secretly
   be married

USING YOUR REASON

7. In a duel, Mercutio believes that Romeo
   (A) will defeat Tybalt (B) will be no match for Tybalt
   (C) should battle Tybalt with words (D) can learn formal
   fencing behavior

IDENTIFYING THE MOOD

8. The overall tone of this scene is
   (A) tender (B) humorous (C) suspenseful (D) gloomy

THINKING IT OVER

1. Shakespeare presents the Nurse as a crude woman who is
   trying to act like a lady. What unladylike qualities does
   the Nurse reveal in this scene? Give examples to support
   your answers.
2. During the "duel of words" between Romeo and
   Mercutio, what kind of mood does Romeo seem to be in?
   How has his mood changed from earlier scenes?

ACT II, Scene 5

FINDING THE MAIN IDEA

1. Which line(s) spoken by Juliet best summarize her goal
   in this scene?
   (A) "I' faith, I am sorry that thou art not well."
   (B) "What says he of our marriage? What of that?"
   (C) "In half an hour she promised to return." (D) "Where
   is my mother? Why, she is within."

REMEMBERING DETAIL

2. How many hours late is the Nurse?
   (A) one (B) two (C) three (D) four
3. The Nurse keeps Juliet waiting while she complains about
   (A) her aches and pains (B) the weather (C) Mercutio's
   bad manners (D) Juliet's mother
4. In this play, "shrift" is the word used to mean
   (A) church (B) balcony (C) confession (D) cell

DRAWING CONCLUSIONS

5. You can figure that the Nurse's teasing
   (A) annoys Juliet (B) amuses Juliet (C) relieves the tension Juliet feels (D) will cause her to be fired

USING YOUR REASON

6. Why does Juliet send Peter away?
   (A) to help Romeo carry out the plan (B) to help ensure
   the secret remains a secret (C) she does not approve of
   him (D) to get the rope ladder

IDENTIFYING THE MOOD

7. Which is probably not a word to describe Juliet's
   feelings while waiting for the Nurse to return?
   (A) hopeful (B) anxious (C) calm (D) nervous
8. Which word most likely describes Juliet's feeling after
   hearing Romeo's instructions?
   (A) sadness (B) fear (C) anger (D) joy

THINKING IT OVER

1. Although the Nurse teases Juliet, she is still sympathetic
   to Juliet's feelings. How does she show this? Do you

284

think the Nurse's feeling toward Romeo matter at all to Juliet? Explain your answer.

2. Given the Nurse's talkative nature, do you think she will be able to keep Juliet's secret? Explain your answer.

3. Many of the scenes in Act II have taken place in the dark. In your opinion, what does darkness symbolize? Why do you think so?

ACT II, Scene 6

FINDING THE MAIN IDEA

1. The most important thing that happens in this scene is (A) the couple confess their sins (B) the couple reaffirm their love for one another (C) the couple go to be married (D) the Friar blesses the couple's union

REMEMBERING DETAIL

2. The wedding is to take place (A) in the Capulets' orchard (B) on Juliet's balcony (C) in the Friar's cell (D) in the village square

USING YOUR REASON

3. Lines such as, "So smile the heavens upon this holy act/That after hours with sorrow chide us not!" show that the Friar (A) still has doubts about the marriage (B) must pray for the couple (C) believes God will bless the marriage (D) hopes the marriage will not end in divorce

IDENTIFYING THE MOOD

4. In this scene, the Friar seems to feel (A) merry (B) worried (C) angry (D) elated

THINKING IT OVER

1. Although this scene precedes the wedding, it is not a happy one. Romeo's own words foreshadow the doom that is to take place. Read the following words, spoken by Romeo:
"Do thou but close our hands with holy words,
Then love-devouring death do what he dare—
It is enough I may but call her mine."
What is ironic about these words?

Act III, Scene 1

FINDING THE MAIN IDEA

1. The most important thing that happens in this scene is
(A) Mercutio and Tybalt fight over Romeo. (B) Romeo
acts cowardly with Tybalt. (C) Romeo tries to stop a
duel. (D) Tybalt is killed, and Romeo is banished.

REMEMBERING DETAIL

2. Who challenges Mercutio and Benvolio in the public
square?
(A) Romeo (B) Paris (C) Tybalt (D) Capulet
3. Mercutio is killed
(A) as Romeo was trying to stop the fight
(B) by Romeo (C) by Paris (D) because he broke the
Prince's law
4. As Mercutio lay dying, he
(A) forgave the man who killed him (B) cursed the
Montagues and Capulets (C) called for Friar Laurence
(D) asked Romeo to avenge him

USING YOUR REASON

5. When Mercutio says, "No, 'tis not so deep as a well, nor
so wide as a church door; but 'tis enough, 'twill serve,"
he means
(A) his wound is serious enough to kill him (B) his
wound is only a scratch (C) that a better duelist would
have done a better job (D) Tybalt is a rat

DRAWING CONCLUSIONS

6. When this scene ends, you can conclude that
(A) a tragic ending is unavoidable now (B) the curse on
the Capulets and the Montagues will come true
(C) Romeo will run away (D) two of these

IDENTIFYING THE MOOD

7. This scene is full of
(A) love and romance (B) sadness and regret (C) happness
and forgiveness (D) violence and hatred

1. How does Mercutio's character remain the same even as he dies?
2. Did Romeo have another course of action than the one he took? Explain. What might have resulted from this choice?

Act III, Scene 2

FINDING THE MAIN IDEA
1. The most important outcome in Act III, Scene 2 is
(A) that Juliet learned of Paris's death (B) Romeo and Juliet planned to leave Verona together (C) Juliet arranged to see Romeo one last time (D) the Capulets exile Romeo

REMEMBERING DETAIL
2. What news does the Nurse give Juliet?
(A) Romeo is dead. (B) Mercutio is dead. (C) Tybalt is dead. (D) Paris is dead.
3. How does Juliet react when she first heard the Nurse's news?
(A) Juliet condemned Romeo (B) Juliet condemned Tybalt (C) Juliet burst into tears (D) Juliet ran to Friar Laurence
4. What does Juliet want the Nurse to take to her "true knight"?
(A) a rope ladder (B) a letter (C) a ring (D) the key to her room

USING YOUR REASON
5. What word would Juliet like to forget when she said these lines, "Some word there was, worser than Tybalt's death,/ That murdered me. I would forget it fain;/ But O, it presses to my memory/ Like damned guilty deeds to sinners' minds!"
(A) *Tybalt* (B) *Romeo* (C) *marriage* (D) *banished*

DRAWING CONCLUSIONS
6. Which of the following statements reflects Juliet's feelings after she learned what had happened in the public square?
(A) Her loyalties originally were divided. (B) She realized

288

the depth of her love for Romeo. (C) She recognized her duty as a wife. (D) all of the above

IDENTIFYING THE MOOD

7. Juliet's soliloquy at the beginning of Scene 2 lets you see her mood. What is it?
(A) happiness (B) sadness (C) mourning (D) impatience

THINKING IT OVER

1. Explain the evidence you have in this scene to show that Juliet is courageous and is growing in maturity.

Act III, Scene 3

FINDING THE MAIN IDEA

1. The most important event in Scene 3 is
(A) Romeo and the Friar develop a plan of action
(B) Romeo is very upset (C) The Nurse thinks Romeo's behavior is immature (D) The Friar scolds Romeo

REMEMBERING DETAIL

2. With whom does Romeo take refuge after the fight in the public square?
(A) the Montagues (B) Benvolio (C) Juliet (D) Friar Laurence

3. What does Romeo feel about his punishment?
(A) It is worse than death. (B) He feels relieved.
(C) He thinks it is fair. (D) He wants to appeal the sentence.

4. What does Romeo threaten to do after the Nurse tells of Juliet's grief?
(A) kidnap Juliet (B) kill himself (C) challenge the Prince to a duel (D) two of these

USING YOUR REASON

5. Why is the Friar so willing to help Romeo?
(A) The Friar hopes to end the feud. (B) Friar Laurence is Romeo's cousin. (C) He believes it is God's will.
(D) The Friar considers Romeo his son.

DRAWING CONCLUSIONS

6. Romeo's long speech to the Friar about banishment reveals that he is
   (A) rash (B) impetuous (C) highly emotional (D) all of these

IDENTIFYING THE MOOD

7. Romeo's speech
   > Yet "banished"? Hang up philosophy!
   > Unless philosophy can make a Juliet,
   > Displant a town, reverse a prince's doom,
   > It helps not, it prevails not. Talk no more.

   helps to create what tone in this scene?
   (A) quiet (B) intense (C) dark (D) joyous

THINKING IT OVER

1. In Scene 2 and Scene 3 you have seen how Romeo and Juliet react to bad news. Compare and contrast the ways the two handle their grief. Who do you think handles it better?

Act III, Scene 4

FINDING THE MAIN IDEA

1. This scene is
   (A) a romantic conversation between Romeo and Juliet
   (B) set in Mantua (C) unimportant to the play
   (D) another example of fate at work

REMEMBERING DETAIL

2. Capulet decides that
   (A) He and Lady Capulet will renew their marriage vows
   (B) Juliet must enter a convent (C) Romeo is welcome as his son-in-law (D) Juliet and Paris will marry
3. The ceremony will take place on
   (A) Tuesday (B) Wednesday (C) Thursday (D) Friday

USING YOUR REASON

4. Capulet's decision in this scene contradicts his decision to (A) divorce Lady Capulet (B) bury Tybalt in the Capulet tomb (C) disown Juliet (D) let Juliet agree to marriage

DRAWING CONCLUSIONS

5. Why does Capulet say, "I will make a desperate tender/ Of my child's love."
   (A) He hopes he can stop Juliet's grieving by arranging a wedding. (B) He wants Juliet's out of the house.
   (C) He is ashamed of Juliet's behavior (D) He wants to see Juliet happy before he dies.

IDENTIFYING THE MOOD

6. Capulet's decision that the ceremony will take place in three days increases the feeling of
   (A) tragedy (B) happiness (C) danger (D) haste

THINKING IT OVER

7. Do you think Romeo's and Juliet's troubles result from fate? Explain why you think so.

Act III, Scene 5

FINDING THE MAIN IDEA

1. This scene makes Juliet more desperate and a tragic end more unavoidable because
   (A) Juliet now hates Romeo (B) Juliet can no longer confide in the Nurse or expect sympathy from her parents (C) Juliet decides to poison herself to avoid marriage with Paris (D) her parents kicked her out of the house

REMEMBERING DETAIL

2. Romeo leaves Juliet's room
   (A) at midnight (B) at dawn (C) at noon (D) in the afternoon
3. Lady Capulet wants Juliet to
   (A) help avenge Mercutio's death (B) help her poison Romeo (C) marry Benvolio (D) divorce Romeo

4. When Juliet refuses to marry, Capulet threatens
(A) to send her to a convent (B) to tie her up and carry
her to the church (C) throw her out of the house
(D) a beating and imprisonment

USING YOUR REASON

5. Which of the following is not an example of dramatic irony?
(A) "Yet let me weep for such a feeling loss" (B) "And
no man like he doth grieve my heart" (C) Out, you baggage!/ You tallow-face!" (D) "Would none but I might
venge my cousin's death"

DRAWING CONCLUSIONS

6. What do Capulet's words calling Juliet "green-sickness
carrion," " young baggage," and "disobedient wretch"
reveal about his character?
(A) He has a temper. (B) He loves his daughter. (C) He is
jealous of Romeo. (D) He fears for Juliet's life.

IDENTIFYING THE MOOD

7. At the beginning of this scene, the lovers are talking to
one another, and the mood is
(A) loud and furious, (B) joyful and happy (C) angry and
silly (D) quiet and anxious

8. In the second part of the scene as Juliet's parents tell her
of her coming marriage, the mood changes to
(A) loud and furious, (B) joyful and happy (C) angry and
silly (D) quiet and anxious

THINKING IT OVER

1. How has the Nurse's role changed in this scene? What
difference do you predict it will make?

ACT IV, Scene 1

FINDING THE MAIN IDEA

1. The most important thing that happens in this scene is
   (A) Paris asks Friar Lawrence to perform the wedding
   (B) Friar Lawrence tries to talk Paris out of marrying Juliet
   (C) Friar Lawrence and Juliet devise a plan to stop the wedding from happening (D) Juliet agrees to marry Paris

REMEMBERING DETAIL

2. When Juliet enters the Friar's cell, Paris addresses her as
   (A) "my sweet love" (B) my "unstained wife"
   (C) my "pensive daughter" (D) "my lady and my wife"
3. Juliet tells Friar Lawrence that, before marrying Paris, she would rather
   (A) leap from a tower (B) lurk among serpents (C) neither A nor B (D) both A and B
4. Juliet tells the Friar she will drink his potion without fear or doubt in order to
   (A) "live an unstained wife to my sweet love" (B) "stop the inundation of her tears" (C) "be married to this County" (D) "go into a new-made grave"

USING YOUR REASON

5. The Friar's aside, "I would I knew not why it should be slowed," means
   (A) he doesn't want an explanation of why there should be a speedy marriage (B) he wishes he had no knowledge of or involvement in the matter (C) he still cannot understand why Capulet cannot wait (D) he wishes he had the power to stop the wedding
6. Which line(s) express that Juliet will kill herself with a dagger before marrying Paris?
   (A) "I will confess to you that I love him." (B) "Come weep with me—past hope, past care, past help!"
   (C) "Love give me strength, and strength shall help afford." (D) "Give me some present counsel; or, behold,/'Twixt my extremes and me this bloody knife/Shall play the umpire. . . ."

DRAWING CONCLUSIONS

7. You can conclude from Paris' words that
   (A) he is marrying Juliet only because Capulet wants him to (B) he sincerely loves Juliet (C) he wants Juliet to marry Romeo (D) none of the above

IDENTIFYING THE MOOD

8. What is Juliet's mood as she speaks to Friar Lawrence?
   (A) desperate (B) cheerful (C) mocking (D) romantic

THINKING IT OVER

1. Does Juliet show a new maturity and new sense of determination in this scene? Find examples from the scene that provide evidence of this new maturity and determination.
2. How will Juliet be affected if there is no way to postpone the wedding? Predict what she might do if she cannot get out of marrying Paris.

ACT IV, Scene 2

FINDING THE MAIN IDEA

1. The main thing that happens in this scene is
   (A) Capulet hires twenty cooks for the wedding
   (B) Juliet apologizes to Capulet and tells him she will marry Paris (C) Juliet and the Nurse choose the clothes Juliet will be married in (D) Juliet and Paris get married

REMEMBERING DETAIL

2. Capulet refers to Juliet's disobedience as
   (A) a "dismal scene" (B) an "inconstant toy" (C) a "peevish self-willed harlotry" (D) a "horrible conceit of death"
3. Which line does Juliet not use in apologizing to her father?
   (A) "Pardon, I beseech you!" (B) "My heart is wondrous light,/Since this same wayward girl is so reclaimed."

(C) "Henceforward I am ever ruled by you." (D) "I have learned me to repent the sin/Of disobedient opposition. . ."

USING YOUR REASON
4. What does Capulet mean by "I'll have this knot knit up tomorrow morning."?
(A) He'll have the feast prepared in the morning
(B) He'll make sure Juliet's clothes are sewed up by morning (C) He'll put off punishing Juliet till the morning (D) He'll arrange for the wedding to take place on Wednesday morning instead of Thursday.

DRAWING CONCLUSIONS
5. When Capulet says, "This is as't should be," you can figure that he
(A) believes Juliet's apology is sincere (B) is skeptical about Juliet's intentions (C) is still angry at Juliet
(D) accepts Juliet's decision not to marry Paris

IDENTIFYING THE MOOD
6. Capulet's mood after Juliet apologizes is
(A) angry (B) sullen (C) merry (D) sarcastic

THINKING IT OVER
1. Why does Juliet not protest when Capulet decides to change the wedding from Thursday to Wednesday? What does she know that her father doesn't know?
2. In your opinion, is Juliet's plan a good one? Would it be more logical for her to simply tell her family the truth? Explain your answer.

ACT IV, Scene 3

FINDING THE MAIN IDEA
1. The most important thing that happens in this scene is
(A) Juliet prays for forgiveness (B) Juliet talks to her mother before going to bed (C) Juliet confides in the Nurse (D) Juliet drinks the sleeping potion

REMEMBERING DETAIL

2. To make sure she is alone in her bedroom, Juliet asks the Nurse to
(A) sit with Lady Capulet (B) remain outside Juliet's door (C) go to fetch Paris (D) help Capulet with the wedding arrangements

3. Juliet's last words, before drinking the sleeping potion, are
(A) "Farewell! God knows when we shall meet again."
(B) "I pray thee leave me to myself tonight."
(C) "Romeo, Romeo, Romeo, I drink to thee." (D) "Stay, Tybalt, stay!"

USING YOUR REASON

4. Juliet's soliloquy reveals that she
(A) is frightened by what she is about to do (B) is not afraid of what will happen after she drinks the potion (C) has lost her mind (D) distrusts the Friar

DRAWING CONCLUSIONS

5. On several occasions, Juliet mentions using a dagger to end her life. You can tell from this that she
(A) is obsessed with daggers (B) is bluffing in the hope that her parents will realize how much she loves Romeo (C) is not serious about ending her life (D) is determined to die before marrying Paris

IDENTIFYING THE MOOD

6. The tone of this scene is
(A) comic (B) hostile (C) festive (D) joyless

THINKING IT OVER

1. After considering all of the possible horrors that could result from drinking the sleeping potion, would you say that Juliet is foolish or courageous to drink it? Explain your opinion.

ACT IV, Scene 4

FINDING THE MAIN IDEA

1. In this scene, the Capulets are
(A) cursing the Montagues (B) preparing for Juliet's funeral (C) preparing for Juliet's wedding (D) getting ready to go to Mass

2. Who calls Capulet a "mouse hunt"?
(A) the Nurse (B) Lady Capulet (C) the First Fellow
(D) the Second Fellow
3. At the end of the scene, Capulet orders the Nurse to
(A) take spices into the kitchen (B) bring dates and
quinces into the pastry (C) go to bed (D) go waken Juliet

USING YOUR REASON
4. Capulet is not tired because he is
(A) excited (B) well-rested (C) young (D) about to be married

DRAWING CONCLUSIONS
5. The reason Shakespeare included this scene was to
(A) present this cheery atmosphere as irony and contrast
to the tragic reality of this drama (B) present the Nurse in
a more lighthearted spirit (C) introduce the First and
Second Fellows (D) provide the audience with hope of a
happy ending

IDENTIFYING THE MOOD
6. The mood of this scene is
(A) dismal (B) tense (C) festive (D) somber

THINKING IT OVER
1. Predict how the atmosphere of the Capulet household
will change after the Nurse goes to awaken Juliet.

ACT IV, Scene 5

FINDING THE MAIN IDEA
1. The important discovery made in this scene is that
(A) Juliet is "dead" (B) the wedding has been postponed
(C) Romeo is dead (D) Juliet drank the sleeping potion

REMEMBERING DETAIL
2. Lady Capulet describes the day of Juliet's "death" as
(A) "accursed" (B) "unhappy" (C) "wretched" (D) all of
the above
3 Capulet laments that wedding cheer has turned to
(A) "a sad burial feast" (B) "melancholy bells"
(C) "sullen dirges" (D) "solemn hymns"

4. Peter asks the musicians to play
   (A) a solemn hymn (B) "Blooming Roses" (C) "Heart's Ease" (D) "The Wedding March"

USING YOUR REASON

5. When the Friar tells Capulet, "The heavens do low'r upon you for some ill," the ill the Friar is hinting at is probably
   (A) Capulet's part in the ongoing feud (B) Capulet's mistreatment of Juliet (C) Capulet's former womanizing (D) Capulet's poor manners
6. Most of the wordplay at the end of the scene involves
   (A) love (B) marriage (C) music (D) death

DRAWING CONCLUSIONS

7. You can conclude that the person least saddened by Juliet's "death" is
   (A) Capulet (B) Lady Capulet (C) Paris (D) the Friar

IDENTIFYING THE MOOD

8. The overall tone of this scene is
   (A) joyous (B) sorrowful (C) humorous (D) suspenseful
9. The mood at the end of the scene is
   (A) comic (B) sad (C) affectionate (D) quiet

THINKING IT OVER

1. Describe Friar Lawrence's character. Why do you think he creates his plan rather than tell the Capulets that he has already married Romeo and Juliet?
2. As he enters Juliet's room, Friar Lawrence says, "Come, is the bride ready to go to church?" What makes this question so ironic? Why is he able to calmly and easily offer consolation to the Capulets?

ACT V, Scene 1

FINDING THE MAIN IDEA

1. The most important thing that happens in this scene is
   (A) Romeo has a strange dream (B) Romeo learns of
   Juliet's "death" and vows to join her in death (C) Romeo
   goes to an apothecary (D) Romeo speaks with Balthasar

REMEMBERING DETAIL

2. In Romeo's dream, his lady finds him
   (A) singing (B) weeping (C) sleeping (D) dead
3. Juliet is buried in
   (A) Mantua (B) the Friar's cell (C) the Capulets' orchard
   (D) Capels' monument
4. How much money does Romeo offer the apothecary?
   (A) forty ducats (B) forty dollars (C) forty drams
   (D) forty cents

USING YOUR REASON

5. When Balthasar speaks of Juliet's "immortal part," he is
   referring to her
   (A) body (B) soul (C) personality (D) none of these
6. Romeo challenges fate when he utters the words
   (A) "Ah me! How sweet is love itself possessed."
   (B) "No matter. Get thee gone." (C) "Is it e'en so? Then I
   defy you, stars!" (D) "Well, Juliet, I will lie with thee
   tonight."

DRAWING CONCLUSIONS

7. Balthasar pleads with Romeo to have patience, saying,
   "Your looks are pale and wild and do import some misadventure." He probably knows that Romeo is
   (A) about to do something foolish (B) sick (C) thinking
   about another girl (D) thinking clearly
8. You can conclude that, in the end, the apothecary was
   most concerned about
   (A) upholding the law (B) saving Romeo's life
   (C) ending his poverty (D) helping his fellow man

IDENTIFYING THE MOOD
9. What is Romeo's mood as the scene opens?
   (A) angry (B) sad (C) tense (D) happy
10. After learning of Juliet's "death," Romeo feels
    (A) sadness (B) anger (C) both A and B (D) neither A nor B

THINKING IT OVER
1. Upon learning of Juliet's "death," Romeo decides he must die, too. How is this decision typical of Romeo? What does it say about his nature?
2. The apothecary Romeo chooses is tattered and poor. Why does Romeo choose this particular apothecary? How does Romeo persuade the apothecary to sell him poison?

ACT V, Scene 2

FINDING THE MAIN IDEA
1. The purpose of this scene is to reveal that
   (A) Juliet is buried alive in a tomb (B) the plague is spreading through Verona (C) Friar Lawrence's letter never reaches Romeo (D) Juliet will awaken from the dead in three hours

REMEMBERING DETAIL
2. Friar John is quarantined, along with
   (A) Friar Lawrence (B) Romeo (C) his servant
   (D) a barefoot brother
3. In stressing the importance of his letter to Romeo, Friar Lawrence refers to it as being
   (A) "not nice" (B) "full of charge" (C) "of dear import"
   (D) all of the above

USING YOUR REASON
4. Friar Lawrence will use an "iron crow" to open Juliet's tomb. An iron crow is a
   (A) kind of hammer (B) large bird made of cast iron
   (C) crowbar (D) pickaxe

300

DRAWING CONCLUSIONS

5. You can figure that, if anything bad happens to Romeo or Juliet, Father Lawrence will
   (A) kill himself (B) not be affected (C) hold himself responsible (D) pray for them

IDENTIFYING THE MOOD

6. In this scene, Friar Lawrence probably feels
   (A) frantic (B) carefree (C) hostile (D) playful

THINKING IT OVER

1. In the first scene of this Act, Romeo asked his servant, "Hast thou no letters to me from the friar?" If the answer had been "yes," how might this scene and the play have ended differently?
2. What new plan does Friar Lawrence devise at the end of the scene? Do you think this plan will work? Why or why not?

ACT V, Scene 3

FINDING THE MAIN IDEA

1. The most important thing that happens in this scene is
   (A) Romeo kills Paris (B) Romeo places Paris' body in Juliet's tomb (C) Romeo and Juliet kill themselves
   (D) Friar Lawrence exposes the lovers' secret marriage

REMEMBERING DETAIL

2. Romeo tells his servant that he has two reasons for entering Juliet's tomb. One is to behold her face once more. The other is to
   (A) desecrate her body (B) desecrate Tybalt's body
   (C) take a ring from her finger (D) kiss her lips
3. The line, "Condemnèd villain, I do apprehend thee," is spoken by
   (A) Romeo (B) Balthasar (C) Paris (D) Paris' page
4. Before drinking the poison, Romeo promises Juliet that he will
   (A) "... lie discolored by this place of peace" (B) "... die with a restorative" (C) "nightly ... strew thy grave and weep" (D) "stay with thee/And never from this pallet of dim night/Depart again"

USING YOUR REASON

5. When Romeo says, "thou womb of death, . . ./I'll cram thee with more food," the food he is talking about is (A) Paris' body (B) his body (C) Juliet's body (D) his salty tears

6. Whose testimony can be considered a synopsis of most of the play? (A) the Friar's (B) Balthasar's (C) Paris' page's (D) the Prince's

DRAWING CONCLUSIONS

7. The sentence that best summarizes the theme of this play is (A) True love never dies. (B) Hate destroys the things that are most precious to people. (C) Relationships should not be entered into hastily. (D) Only mature adults should get married.

IDENTIFYING THE MOOD

8. Upon learning of their children's deaths, the Capulets and the Montagues mostly feel (A) hatred (B) tension (C) excitement (D) grief

9. At the end of this play, the audience should feel (A) happy (B) depressed (C) enlightened (D) afraid

THINKING IT OVER

1. Does the tragedy of this play involve only Romeo and Juliet, or are others affected? Who else is affected by the events of this play?

2. How does the Prince feel that he himself has been punished in this tragedy? Why does he partly blame himself for the lovers' deaths?

3. Which do you believe was more responsible for the tragedy of this play, one or more of the characters or fate? If you believe characters were mostly responsible, tell which character(s) were responsible, and how their actions brought about the tragedy. If you believe fate played the bigger role in this tragedy, tell briefly how fate was responsible. In either case, select episodes from the play to support your answers.

302